Mountains, Radio Waves and a Love Letter

Shinji Yoshikawa

Leadstart
INKSTATE

ISBN 978-93-5667-269-7

First published in India 2023 by Leadstart Inkstate
A brand of One Point Six Technologies Pvt. Ltd.

Unit no. 26, Ground Floor, A1, Shram Safalya,
Wadala Truck Terminal Road, Near Post Office,
Antop Hill, Mumbai – 400037.
Phone: +91 96999 33000
Email: info@leadstartcorp.com
www.leadstartcorp.com

Editor: Vaibhav Pathare
Cover: R. Maharaja
Layouts: Sathish Kumar

One's destination is never a place,
but a new way of seeing things.

Henry Miller

From Mexico City to Chiapas

The state of Chiapas is located approximately 750 km southeast of the densely populated metropolis that is Mexico City. Chiapas is one of my favorite destinations in Mexico, where you can view intricate hand-woven folk art, savor the wonderful aroma of the local coffee beans as well as taste the delicious regional cuisine. Step into a rural village within Chiapas and you will hear the local people speaking not only in Spanish to foreign visitors but also in the ancient Mayan language, which they use to converse amongst themselves. Travelers can also enjoy a cup of freshly prepared regional coffee.

It is here that these fortunate coffee lovers from around the globe can sit back and enjoy their cup of Joe without having to endure the bland ear polluting music that international coffee shop chains so love to play. Silence is golden.

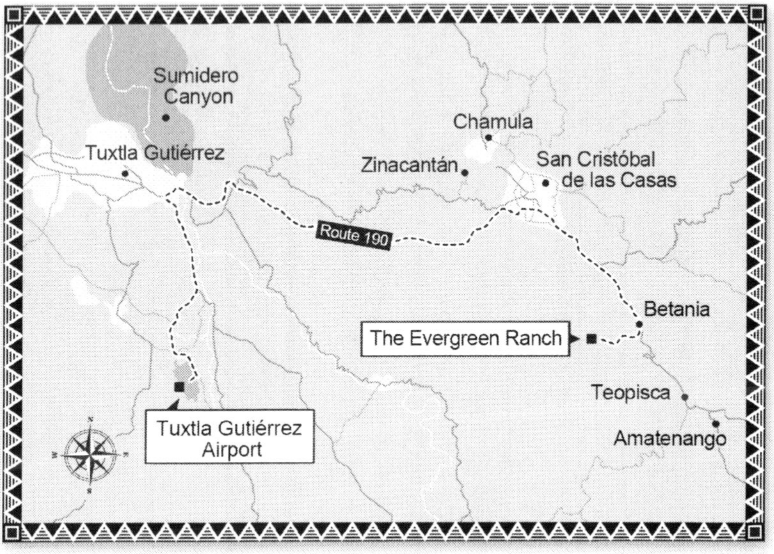

The Evergreen Ranch (El Rancho Evergreen)

If you go further from the city of San Cristobal de las Casas, one of the most indigenous cities in the state of Chiapas, you will be happy to discover a vast ranch. In this picturesque setting, you can experience horse riding during your stay, which attracts many travelers from Europe and other countries from across the globe. You can find this place on TripAdvisor rated with a full mark of 5 (the highest) by the travelers' reviews. I have always wanted to visit this place, and happily, for me, I could finally make the trip.

Contents

Chapter One

Fly to Chiapas

-01-

A Challenge from Chiapas

The directions I received by email from the Evergreen Ranch started like this. "If you come directly from the nearest airport, Tuxtla Gutierrez, you can take a taxi for two hours for 1,000 pesos (about 6,000 yen). But you can also come by bus or shared taxi."

This is followed by a detailed description of how to find a cab or local bus in any village. The village of San Isidro Chichihuistan is located in the Teopisca region of Chiapas, southeast Mexico. A large ranch there is the destination of this trip. It is called "Evergreen" in English because the ranchers are an American and French couple. In Spanish it is called El Rancho Evergreen.

I live in Mexico City, the capital of Mexico, where I work for a Japanese company and live with my family, but it was during the winter of 2018 at Christmas time that I decided to make this trip. My wife and two daughters decided to go to Japan for the winter break, leaving me abandoned during the festive season. During their absence, I had four consecutive days off, which is rare in this country. That is Christmas Eve, Christmas Day, and the Saturday and Sunday before that. But at home in Mexico City, it is cold at this time of year. A chill fills the air, but for me, considering economics, it is not worth turning on the heater only for myself. What is more, being home alone, combined with the low temperatures, would make me feel lonely. So, I decided to travel to the trickiest and most remote place to go, where I know I'll get a kick out of the whole adventure. After contemplating where to go on this escapade, "The Evergreen Ranch" came to mind.

This ranch appeared just once in the travel magazine "México Desconocido", which introduces hidden places to travel to in Mexico. I had purchased every issue of the magazine for over five years till then, and I noticed that most of the popular spots kept popping up every two years or so. One day they would be in the "Top 10 Beach Resorts for Couples" section, the next it's in the "Hidden Beach Spots" section with a different photo. However, this ranch was unusual and showed up only once, and the American kind of name, "Evergreen", stood out from the crowd of other hidden destinations. According to the article, the husband and wife co-owners of the ranch have two children, both girls. They are in their mid-teens, similar to my daughters. They grew up in Mexico, speaking French, English, and Spanish fluently. They and my two daughters have the same backbone, that is, they grew up in Mexico with foreign parents. Hopefully, I would get to know this family. I could envisage the four girls playing happily together in the future. In addition, there are many horses on the ranch and you can learn to ride them. This is one activity that I have always wanted to do.

According to the photos on the ranch's website, the cottages on view look traditional and the animals are cared for by the family. To get there, you first have to go to San Cristobal de las Casas or simply "San Cristobal" a village in the state of Chiapas, where you can find many indigenous people who continue to live in a traditional way, and then drive for another hour.

"If you are going by public transport, when you arrive in the town of San Cristobal, walk to the central market. From there you can take a bus to the nearby villages, and when you get off in the village of Nazareth you can take a shared taxi."

It was quite a hassle as well as time-consuming to have to make all these connections. But the owner of the guesthouse, who at the time didn't know what kind of person I was, a hippy, perhaps a rich guy, a poor student, young or old, emailed me with these options. If you charter a taxi from the airport and pay about 6,000 Japanese yen, it will take you to the ranch deep in the mountains. But "if you take the public bus normally used by the villagers then a shared taxi, it costs 1,800 yen," it says. In the eight years I've lived in Mexico City as an expatriate for a Japanese company, my occasional trips have been mainly to the beach, where I've always been accompanied by a transfer from the airport to my hotel. In addition to the cost of accommodation, flights, and meals, I've always opted for the all-inclusive style. As I've become more and more resort-oriented, I took it upon myself to read the directions from the Evergreen Ranch as a kind of challenge. The information I received gave me food for thought.

"It may be a little difficult for you to come for the first time, but most travelers get here by bus or shared taxi. We usually share taxis with people in our village. But if you are rich enough, you can get a taxi directly from the airport."

It didn't say so directly like that, but this message made me think that it was impossible to take a taxi directly from the airport to the ranch from the point of view of "The Evergreen common sense". This encouragement to guests to save money is clearly reflected in the price categories of the rooms. The Barn Wood Room, where I stayed, has three beds, and the price was 250 pesos (1,500 yen) per night for a bed, 400 pesos (2,400 yen) for two beds, and 700 pesos (4,200 yen) if you rent the whole room.

I took a look at the pictures on their website and it looked like an old-style crafted hut, built from wood from the village. "The Cottage", the other one was already booked up, even though it was a month and a half away before my trip.

"Many of our guests stay here for a long time, so most of them share their rooms with other travelers. If you wish to pay extra, you can rent a whole room for yourself. What would you like to do?"

So says the email from the guesthouse. Part of me wanted to stick my neck out and share a room, but ultimately I didn't want to bother any unfortunate roommate with my world-famous snoring and sleep-talking, so luckily for everyone, I decided to rent a whole room for myself. Also, it's still cheaper than any hotel I usually stay in. Arriving at a traditional cottage like this, to my mind it would definitely be more suitable to take a local bus or shared taxi than to arrive directly in a chartered private taxi as it would give me the feeling of a true adventure.

When I was a student in my early twenties, I studied in Mexico for two years. During the school summer holidays, I would take the bus to various places. At that time I never thought of the option of taking a taxi alone. In Mexico City, for example, I always took the metro, and in Oaxaca, the state next to Chiapas, I rode the local buses which was a life experience in itself. Fast approaching a rickety, green bus that belched black exhaust fumes, which would stop anywhere in the street when you raised your forefinger from your right hand. I learned this by imitating the locals. When stopping, I hurried to join the other passengers to squeeze in through the always-open door. Cheaply, I suppose, is how I've always got around.

As time went by and I was about to turn fifty, I could only take three or four days off at the most. I have learned to use this as an excuse to "buy time with money". It sounds poetic, but it's just a fixed way of thinking that makes you give up on the details and hassles which you may encounter. It stuck in my mind like a fatty piece of meat does to your belly and finally, I couldn't get rid of it. But what do I do with the time I have saved? The answer is "nothing special".

-02-

Grumpy Chickens

On the day of departure, the 22nd of December, the first day of a four-day long weekend, I woke up at the silly hour of 4:30 am. With my red eyes still half shut, I got my things together and left my flat in the early morning darkness at 5:15 am.

I always take a taxi to the airport in Mexico City with a familiar driver called Angel. This elderly driver has a very special talent among the unpunctual Mexicans. He arrives at your doorstep five minutes before the appointed time, no matter what happens. Almost every foreigner living in Mexico realizes how difficult it is to make an appointment with a Mexican and be on time the more they live here. Of course, it is not always the case, but often it is at least fifteen minutes late. But this is the norm in Mexico, and if you get frustrated and grumpy about it, then, for sure, this is not the place for you. But when I got to know this strange 'keeper of the time' driver, my long-ingrained fear that the taxi might not be on time disappeared from my life. That fear was about to be settled in my genes and passed on to the next generation.

On the first day of the holidays, even though it was early in the morning at the airport in Mexico City, there was a rush to get out of the country and a long queue at the international check-in counters. The more affluent Mexicans take advantage of this opportunity to fly to Spain or Los Angeles, where their relatives live. Even if you don't want to go abroad, there are many resorts in Mexico to visit, such as the world-famous Cancun and Puerto Vallarta. However, the domestic flights were not the only ones that were hit by delays at this ungodly hour. Due to overbooking by the airlines, a number of unfortunate people traveling further afield were unable to depart on time for their holiday. Fortunately for me, my masterfully chosen Aeromexico flight to Tuxtla Gutierrez left Mexico City on time at 7:15.

Once seated, I slipped into my slippers and pulled up my jumper to my chin as a blanket. I remember the plane taking off with a roar after its runway run-up, but I have no recollection of anything after that. The next thing I knew was that we were preparing to land. I must have fallen asleep immediately after take-off because more than an hour went by without me knowing it. It was a flight without any thrill or excitement at all. I landed at the airport of Tuxtla Gutierrez, my first stopover. I do the same thing on most flights. When my back is pressed against the seat of the accelerating aircraft, I lose consciousness as comfortably as if I were lying on my back on a futon. The early start and the cold medicine I had taken that morning added to the drowsiness.

I thought I hadn't caught a cold this winter, which was unusual, but on the morning of the first day of my trip, which I was looking forward to the most at the very end of the year, I woke up with a nasty sore throat. The cold wave that had hit Mexico in December had been so severe that it ended up taking the lives of people in the northern desert. Even in Mexico City, where my family and I live, the temperature hit two degrees Celsius in the morning, which might be unimaginable for Japanese people who think only of cacti, spicy Don Tacos snacks, and tequila. Despite this cold weather, there is no central heating system in houses or apartments. With north-facing windows, our house is like a refrigerator during the day, so it's hard to get out of bed every morning.

The state of Chiapas, our destination for this trip, is a mosaic of regions with very different climates, from the murderously hot Palenque (where the water in the showers is hotter than your body temperature in summer) to the chilly highlands of San Cristobal, where we will be traveling overland. The city of Tuxtla Gutierrez, the capital of the state, where I landed that day, is at a lower altitude and is one of the hottest. However, as I waited patiently in my seat for the small bus that was going to take me from the airport to San Cristobal to fill up, I felt quite chilly. In the south of the country, like here in Tuxtla Gutierrez, the windows are always open when the engine is not running, probably because of the year-round humidity. Apart from cold-intolerant people like me, most people were wearing only a T-shirt.

By the way, the price of this bus was 200 pesos (1,200 yen), which was even cheaper than the 250 pesos mentioned in the Evergreen Ranch's introduction. I was determined to follow the Evergreen Ranch's financial advice on this solo trip, so this 50 pesos saving was a secret pleasure for me. This time, I didn't look at the luxurious and spacious charter bus sitting next to us but decided to go for the more economical one. Although it had a capacity of 15 people, it seemed to be crammed with anyone who wanted to get on. Moreover, as the local bus is mainly used by locals rather than foreign tourists, their baggage is intensely large. The belongings of European backpackers seemed to be so small, and I found I was surrounded by large suitcases of the locals who work outside of town and were coming back to their hometown for Christmas. If there is so much luggage, the rear seats could be folded down and used for luggage storage, but from a business point of view, this is not allowed because the only way to make a profit is to cram in as many passengers as possible. Bags and the like can occupy the space without paying anything. This is what the attendants are always calculating.

In these situations, I always try to sit next to the driver. When I take a taxi with my family, I usually end up sitting next to the driver. The three ladies in my family fit comfortably in the back seat, so there is an unspoken rule that I, being the man of the house, must sit in the passenger seat. There are a few things I've noticed over the years. First of all, drivers often leave coke bottles, towels, newspapers, and other things in the passenger seat, forgetting or not caring that passengers will be sitting there at some point. This bus also started with passengers crammed into the back of the bus. That's why few people have the chance to get into the passenger seat from the beginning. There are many advantages to such a prized seat. For example, you can enjoy the view from the windscreen and hear the driver talk about the local delicacies. And if the air conditioning is at hand, you can turn it on or off at will. This is important for me because I don't enjoy artificial climates. Best of all though, there's plenty of space.

As it was already my habit to do, I didn't obey the staff's suggestion to sit in the back of the bus and got into the passenger seat. I sat down and waited for about twenty minutes, looking out of the window, but our chariot was still half empty. I was supposed to be enjoying the coolness of the morning, but I was ready to blow a fuse and wondered if the bus would leave any time soon. Then, to my complete joy, my prayers were finally answered. As the other planes arrived, the seats started to fill up, one by one. Finally, all the seats were taken, and as we were about to depart, a slim man leading the passengers to our bus from the airport exit said something I hadn't expected at all.

"I'm sorry sir, can I seat this lady in that middle seat in between?"

By "in-between", he meant the narrow extra seat between the driver and me. It's a seat that wouldn't normally be used. Horror struck my weary frame. I loathed his idea of making a passenger sit in a seat so small that half a man's butt (my own) would hang over the edge of it. What is more, they still charge the same fee for it. The poor young lady who came along apologetically was squeezed into this small seat that the gearshift was sticking out of. That was when my plan to make the bus my own personal oasis for an hour fell apart. I vacated my seat of the tainted vehicle reluctantly to let the short-haired, bright-eyed girl into that middle seat. She has to hold her bag on her lap, with her legs tightly put together, for the whole hour to San Cristobal. I almost felt more sorry for her than for me as a fellow passenger.

As the bus is filled with passengers returning to their hometowns or heading on an adventure, such as I, finally the engine started up for departure. To me, the noise created by the ignition sounded like a Mozart symphony. On the rooftop, the man in charge of strapping down the suitcases looked impatient. He receives the huge suitcases from the muscular ground crew who tosses them up and places them on the roof. After the herculean fellow had made sure that all the luggage was strapped down and secured with heavy-duty ropes, the bus finally set off towards San Cristobal.

The first two-thirds of the way to San Cristobal, my second stop on the way to the ranch, had just a single lane on both sides of the gentle uphill road. On several occasions, our steady progress was blocked by slow-moving trucks. On the other hand, some cars were overtaking much faster than the speed limit. From Tuxtla Gutierrez to San Cristobal and beyond to Comitan and neighboring Guatemala, vehicles of all sizes use this road to transport goods as well as people. When a speeding car comes along, we maneuver to one side to let it go ahead. When our bus was behind a slower-moving car, we needed to move out into the oncoming lane, making sure that no other vehicle was heading towards us, to continue our journey safely.

For a while, a slow-moving truck with a pile of plastic baskets strapped to the back was in front of us. The winding uphill climb made it impossible to see if there was a car in the other lane, so we couldn't risk overtaking it. This meant that we were forced to drive slowly for about 10 minutes. With nothing else to do, I found myself staring at the back of the truck. It was then that I noticed a large number of boxes, each containing a chicken. They were in cream-colored cages with their red beaks on show. The poor beasts were cowering down with fearful eyes, as if to say "please stop driving so wildly, I feel car sick." At a rough count, there were about a hundred and fifty baskets piled up. Each one contains two or three chickens, so there are at least three hundred of the winged serpents on board. The majority of them, I fear, are destined to be plucked, seasoned, and stuffed into an oven sooner rather than later. While I was pondering the fate of these chickens, the conversation between the girl next to me and the driver endlessly went on.

"I'm going to my cousin's wedding," she says. And the driver says, "Well, you should go to the Sumidero Valley because it's beautiful, young lady," and so on.

After the long and leisurely ride in our shared four-wheeled beast, countless pine trees came into view on the mountainside. I found this a nostalgic landscape due to it reminding me of Japan. When Haruki Murakami, the famous Japanese novelist who wrote Tokio Blues (Norwegian Wood) and 1Q84, visited here in the nineties, he wrote that it reminded him of Japan too. After an hour and a half, the trusty bus finally arrived in San Cristobal, a rather sad-looking town dotted with indigenous villages.

-03-

Tangerine Juice and Corn

"When you get off the bus, walk to the central market of San Cristobal and take the bus to the village of Nazareth." I thought I would follow the directions I received from the ranch and walk to the market, but it turned out that I would have to walk ten blocks, maybe a kilometer, according to some friendly local chaps who were there at the stop. To my mind, with only a backpack and a small carry-on case on casters, I could make it, but I wanted to conserve my strength for the long day ahead.

As I lingered at the bus station, I was bombarded with temptations from taxi drivers and bus company men, who told me to relax and hop into their very own trustworthy form of transport. It was as if a witch had offered me a poisoned apple. By this time, I was sure I'd made up my mind to take cheap shared transport this time. If I enjoy it now, my life will be filled with "easy but expensive" things.

I was pacing along the pavement next to the busy road that connects San Cristobal to Teopisca, thinking about this and that, when I saw a lively procession of people in the street. On the back of a truck that was proudly blocking the flow of traffic, young children were dressed as angels with beautiful flowers decorating the vehicle. Behind the little angels, figures of a young Jesus with Mary and Joseph were displayed.

The procession is held to celebrate Christmas. Towering dolls, that were twice the size of the average human, were dressed in traditional clothing. Inside each giant doll, a man was manipulating their movements. The huge figures represent the different races of people from around the world. This symbolized the fact that we are all children of God. To round off the entertainment, a brass band played enthusiastically. Crossing the country road into the center of town, the group carried a statue of a saint on the back of a pick-up truck following behind. Judging by the lack of tourists around, they are genuinely taking the statue out of the church and performing Christmas rituals to the sound of a local brass band playing trumpets and drums. What impressed me the most in this festive spectacle was the dancing paper mache woman with pigtails, that was over three meters tall, whirling and twirling across the street in front of us, it was a joy to behold.

As I continued to walk in search of a taxi rank where I hoped I would find fellow travelers to share a taxi with, a stall, run by a mother and daughter team, selling tangerine juice and charcoal-grilled corn caught my eye, so I decided to stop for a drink to relieve my parched throat. The corn waiting to be consumed was an unusually dark yellow color but looked delicious, nonetheless. No, rewind, it's not yellow, it's more like orange. It is slowly roasted over a charcoal fire. It cost 15 pesos, which is less than a hundred yen. I also bought some tangerine juice, which they were selling together, and decided to settle down for a while.

In contrast, the corn sold at roadside stalls in Mexico City is cream-colored and large-grained. It's usually covered in a thick layer of mayonnaise and topped with bright red chili powder, lemon, and cheese powder. This stall, on the other hand, serves it simply, with lemon and salt. The stalks are used as handles, and instead of a Styrofoam container, they are served on a corn husk. The yellow-green skin is covered with fuzzy white hairs. Finally, there is a little bit of coarse salt on it, to add to the dining experience. I like the simplicity and naturalness of it. It's eco-friendly.

Moving on from the 3-star Michelin food stall, I came across a pharmacy. It's a chain of pharmacies called "Farmacia del Ahorro", which sells generic drugs. These pharmacies, which are spread all over Mexico, often have small clinics attached to them, staffed by doctors. In return for a free consultation, the prescription will always include a generic drug of the "save money" variety. I love the way that the doctor and the pharmacy depend on each other to survive. Anyway, there are doctors all over the place who will see you for free, without an appointment, giving the public the peace of mind that if their weekly budget is low, no problem. My throat felt quite sore, so I decided to drop in. As I peered into the waiting room, I noticed that the door to the examination room was open. I had hit the jackpot in that no other patients were waiting time at that moment.

I walked into a small, white-walled examination room where a tall, athletic-looking young female Mexican doctor was busy analyzing her mobile phone. Lucky me. Besides, I had already seen a doctor in Mexico City at this "save your money" type clinic. So I was registered in the patient database and didn't have to repeat my name and date of birth from the beginning. After a quick check-up, I only asked for a throat examination and resisted the urge to ask for directions of any sort.

"I'll give you some antibiotics just in case, but only take them if your situation does not improve or becomes worse."

The doctor, who had an attractive, low-pitched voice, said this as she went to her computer and began to type in the names of the drugs she was prescribing. I was relieved to find that my condition was less severe than I had expected. After all, I was about to head further into the mountains and ride horses in the wilderness, and it would be hard to be told to "rest easy". The prescription was printed out and I also got four extra discount coupons for the "Save Money" pharmacy. A win-win situation if ever there was one.

"So, where are you going?"

She asked in a husky voice as if she could see I needed directions.

"I want to go towards Teopisca, but I don't know where I can get a shared taxi."

"Teopisca? There's nothing much to see there."

The doctor sighed a little, not attempting to hide her "what's with the strange Asian" expression.

"But if you want a ride, just walk a little further down the road. You can get a taxi there."

Afterward, she told me that many unexplored places in Chiapas are not yet known. She also likes to travel and when she heard that I was going to the ranch, she told me about her experiences. It was interesting for me to find out that her husband works for the government's tourism ministry, working with the locals to promote ecotourism in the untouched jungle.

"I was taken there once, and it's lovely to visit such an unspoiled environment. There are birds and other forms of wildlife wandering around everywhere without you having to look very hard for them". She and her husband live in Chiapas, but my newly found antibiotic savior is actually from the northern coastline of Mexico. As it turned out, it is not only foreigners who are fascinated by the nature of Chiapas.

To get from San Cristobal to the village of San Isidro Chichihuistan, where the Evergreen Ranch is located, the email I received from the ranch said to take a taxi you can share or failing that, a local bus to Teopisca, the last stop. “Teopisca” is indeed the name of the place which does not appear in the tourist guide, and there is nothing much for foreigners to do there. But for me, it was a landmark that would lead me to my destination. If you take the main road, route 190 towards Teopisca, you will first come to the village of Betania, and then to the village of Nazareth. If you desire to go to San Isidro Chichihuistan, you have to get off at one of the villages. Then, if you are lucky enough to find a taxi you can share waiting for you in Nazareth, you will be able to leave the main road for San Isidro Chichihuistan and reach the ranch in 40 minutes.

I thanked her politely and bought a set of medicines from the “Save Money” pharmacy next door. I took the medicine with some water I had bought and put the bottle and medicine into my backpack. The corn I had purchased earlier at the stall was also there, wrapped in a tissue.

A festival blocks the way in San Cristobal.

-04-

Uncle Rogerio's Ambitions

I went along the road, ruminating on the directions I had been given until I came to a T-junction where six taxis were waiting in a well-behaved queue. This seemed to be the place I was looking for. In the back seat of the first taxi sat a well-tanned couple with large bags on their knees, looking as if they were returning to their village. They were sitting in the back seat of a three-seater, with plenty of room for one more person. This is the etiquette, the rule, of being a passenger in a shared taxi. The exact opposite of the politeness of Japanese high school students and rude middle-aged office workers who put their bags or briefcases on the seat next to them on buses and trains, hoping that no one will come to fill that space. In truth, I am unable to exclude myself from such actions, as I secretly prayed for no one to sit next to me on the bus ride to San Cristobal.

As I wandered around, unsure of whether I was in the right taxi rank, an elderly driver with a hunting cap and mustache exited the driver's seat of his taxi. I was expecting him to call out to me, but instead, he joined in a conversation with a group of young people who were hanging out on the pavement nearby and started chatting amicably. I'm sure he thought that foreign tourists like me wouldn't want to be a passenger in such a shared (or, for lack of a better word, ramshackle) taxi. I had no choice but to call out to him.

"I want to go to Nazareth. Can I catch a shared taxi here?"

"Yes" came his reply. "Get in this one."

As soon as he realized I was a guest, his movements suddenly became more agile. He lifted the black carry-on case that I had carefully pulled along with me and began to push it into the trunk with a lot of force. But it doesn't quite fit because of all the other stuff that's piled up. There are cardboard boxes full of groceries, clothes, and other supplies that the backseat-crammed couple will be taking back to their village. Each piece of luggage has a string crisscrossed haphazardly around it. At this point, I took over the crushing of my case and somehow I managed to squeeze my bag into the gap in the dusty trunk, and finally, I climbed into the passenger seat.

Terror shivered down my spine as the taxi showed no sign of leaving. I thought it was the same pattern as the bus earlier, so I desperately looked around and saw that he was going to wait for as long as he could for other passengers. He seemed to be in no particular hurry, and again he started chatting leisurely with the young people. In short, one more passenger was missing who was going in the same direction. The fare for one person is 35 pesos (200 yen), so it's a matter of life and death for the driver whether or not another person gets on. I've always paid extra money to take a taxi alone, to save waiting time. So, in reality, for now, I have no reason to complain at all.

Finally, to the utmost joy of all of us, the last person, a middle-aged woman who was probably on her way back to her village, arrived like a gift from above, got in and the car finally left. Several taxi drivers had offered to take me to the village of Nazareth for 100 pesos (600 yen). Being a weak man, I was tempted to put aside my original vow and use my sore throat as an excuse to take the more expensive option. But I'm glad I said no. It would have cost me a little extra to take the easy way out. But as time is always in control, I decided for once to sit back and relax and ignore my timepiece. Let the games begin.

"Where do you come from?"

As usual, I sat in the greatly desired passenger seat, and the driver, whose name was Rogerio, inquisitively spoke to me. He doesn't say much, but he asks me a few questions in a simple, choppy tone. It seemed to me that I was a rare foreign passenger for him and he had a lot of questions for me.

"I'm from Japan, but now I live in Mexico City. When I get off at the village of Nazareth, I plan to take another shared taxi to the Evergreen Ranch where I'll stay for 3 or 4 nights."

"Oh, I see. By the way, what's the Japanese currency called?"

Uncle Rogerio stomped on the accelerator and for some reason started talking about money.

"It's a yen."

Like most Mexicans, Uncle Rogerio pronounces 'yen' like 'Jen'.

"How much is the yen to the peso?"

"Nowadays a peso costs about six yen."

"So the peso is more powerful as a currency?"

Well, that's what happens when you compare numbers at conversion rates.

Many times I have had to deal with elderly people in Mexico who ignore the mechanism of exchange rates and simply try to compare "which currency is stronger" based on the size of the numbers. Each time I have tried to explain to them that currency rates change according to the balance of the market, they have not been able to understand, so they tend to take the subject in a completely different direction. I don't have the Spanish language skills to explain economic principles in simple terms.

Uncle Rogerio began to talk about the quetzal, the currency of neighboring Guatemala. Even if each quetzal is 2.5 pesos, it never simply means that the peso is cheaper than the quetzal. Through experience, when this kind of comparison is made, it's time to change the subject.

"You've been to Guatemala?"

"Yes, until about eight kilometers over the border."

Just when I was relieved that we were going to be talking about Guatemala, uncle Rogerio said, "By the way, do you have any Japanese yen?"

I understood then that the reason why he was talking about the yen was to ask me to give him some Japanese yen coins as a souvenir of our exquisite time together.

The taxi was speeding along the well-maintained road. When I glanced at the meter to check the velocity, the needle remained at zero and did not move. At this rate, even if the police did stop him for speeding, he is likely to say, "It's not my fault because the meter doesn't work." The policeman, on the other hand, would probably just say, "Just be more careful not to crash, old-timer."

"Unfortunately, I don't have any coins on me, but the next time I am here I will have something for you."

I replied to end this conversation.

"When will that be?"

"Maybe in a year."

"A year from now, I won't be around."

"No, no, no, you're too young. How old are you?"

"Sixty-five years old."

Amid this exchange, I told him that possibly maybe, if I could return someday, I would gladly bring him a five-yen coin for him to enjoy. His answer to this was unexpected.

"No, I'm not looking for a handout. I have a collection of old peso notes as well as notes from all over the world. So of course I will pay you money to buy some Japanese notes from you."

Hearing those words, I regretted that I hadn't listened to the end of the conversation and had made assumptions about people based on their appearance. Uncle Rogerio was not asking me to give him something for nothing because foreigners are rare. He had been collecting notes over the years with his friends, including some old Mexican banknotes worth over 100,000 yen. In other words, he was a genuine collector.

"I understand. Next time I come back, I'm sure I'll find you at the taxi rank, and then I'll have something interesting for your collection."

Who knows if I'll ever see this taxi driver again, driving passengers around to different villages?

After forty minutes of driving in the direction of Teopisca, I decided to ask him to drop me off in the village of Betania, one village before Nazareth. The way I had learned from the Evergreen Ranch was to go to Nazareth and then change for another taxi.

However, it also said that if I couldn't find a taxi to share there, I would have to wait for a taxi to come by, or go back to Betania and, if possible, take a more expensive private taxi from there. What a palava!!! So, I decided to get off at Betania and hopefully stop any rideshare taxis that passed by on the way. However, if I had no other choice, I would have to take a private taxi.

Uncle Rogerio pulls over onto the dirt shoulder, gets out, opens the trunk of the car, and gently places my small black carry-on case on the ground. In contrast to the buzz of conversation in the taxi, the farewell is rather short but sweet. He has a busy time ahead, for he must now quickly and hopefully carefully take the couple in the back seat, along with the gift from heaven woman and her luggage to their final destinations. Route 190 meandered gently towards Teopisca. Uncle Rogerio started the car up at a brisk pace, sending up a loud cloud of dust into the dry, almost clean air.

Uncle Rogerio's car has a broken speedometer.

Chapter Two

Evergreen

-05-

Betania Village

Along the main road in the village of Betania, there is a long line of stalls selling enticing colored fruit such as tangerines, oranges, bananas, and apples. The radiant fruits were displayed on tiered shelves of wooden boxes. At the bottom, a large dark green wax gourd, a tropical fruit that resembles a pumpkin, stands on the ground, a stark contrast of colors, for sure. If I were here with my family, my daughters would be pestering me to go as soon as I stopped to admire the glorious view that nature had provided. But this time I'm traveling alone, therefore no one is here to disturb this simple pleasure. So I say hello to the shopkeeper asking for permission to take some award-winning photos. What is more, without any playful disturbance from loving daughters, I had the luxury of taking my time with my zoom lens.

After nourishing my creative side, I crossed Route 190 in front of me and asked the taxi drivers who were parked along the road how much they would charge to take me to my destination, the village of San Isidro Chichihuistan. I interrogated three possible chauffeurs, all of whom said it would cost 150 pesos (900 yen). I had hoped that one of them might be willing to undercut the other two, but they were all quoting the same price as if they had a formal agreement. No matter how steep the road among the mountains ahead was, I had traveled the one-and-a-half-hour journey from Tuxtla Gutierrez airport to San Cristobal just for 200 pesos (1,200 yen). I couldn't compromise at all to pay almost the same price for about one-twentieth of the distance. But all the vehicles passing by on this main road in front of me were either trucks carrying goods, or private cars, and no matter how long I waited, there was no sign of a taxi that I could share or a bus.

This sorry state of affairs left me with no choice but to walk to Nazareth, a village further on, where there was supposed to be a taxi rank with taxis you could share with other nomads. So, not for the first time, I started lugging my black carry-on case with castors along the road. I should have followed the directions from the ranch to the village of Nazareth and then got out of the taxi, I thought, remembering the face of Uncle Rogerio, whom I had just said goodbye to. I was in the middle of nowhere. A forest was close to the shoulder of the road. The single-track road went on and on, so it was hard to tell how far I had to walk before I could finally reach the village of Nazareth.

As I start to trudge along, I see a white woman wearing sunglasses standing ahead of me. It seemed as if she was staring straight at me. A foreign-looking person in such a remote place, she might be a tourist like me, aiming for the Evergreen Ranch. But I was not sure if she was looking at me because of her sunglasses. Maybe I'm just self-conscious and just imagining her eyes on me. I turned around to see if she was looking at someone behind me, but there was no one there. I pretended not to notice and tried to walk past her, but then I heard my name, "Shinji?" She said with a big smile on her face. As she smiled, the corners of her mouth rose until they reached their peak and showed off her dazzling white teeth. Ironically, it was me who needed those sunglasses, now.

Slender and poised, dressed in tight, pale blue jeans and a long-sleeved white shirt with a collar, she was Stephanie, the co-owner of the Evergreen Ranch I was aiming for. With her hair pulled back and her Olympic gold medal smile against the blue sky, she looked dashing and cool. She was shopping with her daughter when I met her for the first time by sheer coincidence. On the other side of the road, there was a girl who was about to cross it to our side. It was her second daughter, Cheyenne. She was 14 years old, with white skin and chestnut hair, and freckles on her face, she was slim like her mother and looked much more mature than her age. She was wearing trainers and jeans.

They spoke to me in English. By all accounts, I have a genuine Asian-looking face, so it's unlikely that anyone would think I speak Spanish. Whenever I go to a Latin American tourist destination, I am usually spoken to in broken English. So it was only natural that Stephanie and her daughter Cheyenne would speak to me in English.

"Shinji, I'm about to go back to the ranch, so let's take a taxi together."

Upon breathing in that sweet combination of words, I swear I heard my old friend, Mozart, in the distance.

Then I remembered that she was the one who had ignited my spirit for this economy ridesharing trip. On the last leg of my journey to the ranch, I was at a loss as to how I was going to get there, and this is how I was able to get a shared taxi to take me directly to my destination, the Evergreen Ranch.

"I've been watching you talking to the taxi drivers along the road. Then you turned and walked towards me. So I was wondering where you were going."

Stephanie was looking at me with interest, smiling and waiting for a response at the same time. I was tempted to tell her that I was trying to follow her advice, in taking the cheapest way possible to the Evergreen Ranch but I was too shy to do so.

"I was wondering if there were any shared taxis or buses passing by, because it was very expensive to take a taxi alone, and received the tragic news that I would have to walk to the village of Nazareth before I could find a taxi to share. So I had no choice but to start walking."

I was just being honest, but Stephanie was still grinning as if she had come across someone strange.

"And yet you arrived on time, didn't you?"

I had texted them earlier that I would be arriving at the ranch around two o'clock in the afternoon. That's why Stephanie and Cheyenne had come to Betania an hour earlier to buy some fruit and vegetables. As I had told them in the emails that I was Japanese, they knew who I was immediately. More importantly, it turned out to be a superlative decision on my part to get off at Betania instead of going to Nazareth. Apparently, this trip was turning out to be a lucky one. Stephanie's smile was so bright that my gloomy mood was quickly lifted. In a friendly welcome atmosphere, the taxi headed off in the direction of the ranch, with the boot full of shopping bags and crates filled with the spoils of their shopping.

A row of fruit stalls on the shoulder of Route 190.

-06-

Spanish or English?

On the way, the taxi stopped at a roadside stall on Stephanie's instructions. The road from San Cristobal to Betania is well maintained, but once you get off the road and onto the side, it is ochre sand. There were several stalls on view. Along the main roads in Mexico, there are stalls everywhere, and each place has different things to sell. For example, on the way south from Mexico City to the state of Guerrero, where Acapulco is located, bouquets of roses, about fifty in all, are piled haphazardly on a stand and sold. To the northwest, towards Querétaro, there are many packets of strawberries for sale. And here in Chiapas, along the main road from San Cristobal to Teopisca, I saw several crates for purchase as well as potted cacti for ornamental purposes.

Stephanie and Cheyenne went to a stall about five minutes away from Betania to choose a cactus pot. On the way from the ranch to Betania, they had noticed the stall with the cacti on the roadside. As usual, the stall was stacked with crates. As I knew I couldn't take a cactus home with me, I chatted with the man in the stall while I waited.

"I've been seeing a lot of crates in the stalls all over the place, and you have them here too. Why are there so many for sale?"

"Oh, they are used as boxes for carrying fruit and vegetables. We made them from wood from the mountains around here. We also have handmade chairs. How about one?"

He pointed to a thick forest of trees nearby and told me that the crates cost 30 pesos each. He was very enthusiastic, but of course, I politely declined both the crate and the chair. As I listened to him talk about the crates, I thought of a hardworking father who would buy food supplies in San Cristobal, Tuxtla Gutierrez, and other similar towns, for his not-so-well-off family and put the supplies into boxes and load them up on a pickup truck in large quantities. When it came time to take the supplies back to the village where the family lived, the weight and humidity of the stacked cardboard boxes would have become damaged, so the tangerines would burst open, spilling their juice left, right, and center. But with these crates, no matter how many boxes are stacked, at most only the tangerines unlucky enough to be placed at the bottom of each crate will only be slightly misshapen. If he manages to get them safely to his village, I'm sure that even the wives, who are usually stressed with their men as well as strict with their children, will welcome him with a big smile. A smile that even Stephanie would be proud of.

Before long, Stephanie and Cheyenne had picked out two fist-sized cacti for 40 pesos each. Then we got back into the taxi. The cacti were covered with long thorns, like very fine white whiskers. As usual, I sat in the passenger seat and they sat in the back seat as we drove to the ranch.

On the way, our conversation was still in English.

"My family is back in Japan and it's been a while since I've been able to travel on my own. So I was looking for a place that's a bit further away than I'm used to traveling to and I thought of the Evergreen Ranch. If I like it, I might come back with my family."

"So this is a preview and a test for us."

Stephanie cheered at my words. She is very quick in understanding the context.

But when the person you are speaking to is fluent in English, it can be a bit frustrating to not be able to speak at the same speed. It's like when you press the accelerator but the car doesn't go as fast as you want it to. After all, I've never lived in a country where English is spoken as the official language. So as the taxi rattled slowly up and down the mountain road, I was trying to find the right moment to switch to a little more conversational Spanish.

"By the way, what is the common language in your family?"

"It's English. My husband is a Gringo. But he speaks Spanish too."

"Gringo" is a Mexican slang used jokingly to describe Americans. I have been told that it is a derogatory term that was originally used to refer to the U.S. troops stationed in Mexico as "green go", but has since been morphed into Spanish.

" Stephanie, I've been living in Mexico for eight years now. So it's easier for me to speak Spanish than English."

Switching to Spanish, I confided in her honestly. I had overheard Stephanie speaking very natural Spanish with the taxi drivers and the men at the cactus and crate stalls.

English for me, on the other hand, is like when for the first time in my life I needed to converse with Japanese people from Tokyo, due to my studies and later on in my work life. This may sound strange, but I am Osaka born and naturally speak with a completely different accent from Tokyo-born Japanese. Not only the difference in dialect can be an issue, but also the meaning of some words can be used differently. Therefore, it reminds me of when I speak in English, I have to build up a sentence in my head to a certain extent before I can speak with confidence. It makes me nervous, and if I can't communicate, I lose confidence in my pronunciation. Speaking Spanish, for me, on the other hand, is like using the Kansai dialect used by people born in Osaka, where in fact, words flow rather easily without thinking about them too much. It has a more natural feeling.

"I'm French, so I speak Spanish, which has its roots in Latin, without difficulty. Cheyenne and my eldest daughter, Zoë, speak English, Spanish, and French. My husband Samuel is American, so he mainly speaks English, but he also speaks Spanish, although it's a little rusty."

Stephanie said, switching to Spanish exactly at the same rhythm as in English. When you're traveling, deciding what language you're going to converse in can have a big impact on how well you get on with the locals. If, as in this case, the other person seems to be comfortable in any language, I don't hesitate to ask them to speak in my preferred adopted language, Spanish. In this way, I've obtained the base to enjoy the trip to its fullest without feeling inferior. The fourteen-year-old Cheyenne was listening to our conversation in silence.

After twenty minutes of chatting, the slow-moving taxi soon broke up the asphalt road to reveal a gravel road cut into the mountainside. We slowed down to a crawl through the dusty roads and headed further into the forest. We could see a few houses along the way, but it was more like a gravel road cut through the virgin forest and the occasional cornfield. No cars are passing each other, and of course, there are no lanes.

"The speed limit is 20 km per hour. If you exceed the speed limit, you will be fined 1,000 pesos (6,000 yen)."

We saw several handwritten speed limit wooden signs along the way, but it would be difficult to go faster than that speed on this road. A steep slope with no guardrail is just around the corner.

In the rasping, rumbling taxi, you have to speak deep from your stomach to reach the other person. Due to this, slowly but surely, silence began to dominate the scene as the journey went on. After forty minutes of driving up and down the mountain road from the village of Betania, we suddenly came to a straight road that was wide enough for two cars to pass each other. At last, we seemed to have reached our destination.

"Park at the blue gate. We have a lot of stuff to take out."

Stephanie told the driver. The taxi finally stopped in front of a fence rather than a gate. I handed Stephanie the allotted 40 pesos (240 yen) and helped her to take their bags out of the trunk. If I had taken a taxi alone, it would have cost me more than three times as much. It's not usual to meet the proprietress of a ranch like this along the road, but sometimes it's important to persist in your beliefs.

"Welcome to our home. This is the Evergreen Ranch."

Stephanie told me proudly, still showing her beautiful white teeth.

A stall along the national road selling cacti

-07-

Multinational Zone Deep in the Mountains

The gleaming green hue of the lawn is due to the sun-induced growth of the grass. A few wooden fences roughly divide the vast area. The air seems even clearer than before, perhaps because we've just driven a taxi along a dusty road. The sky was deep blue and I could feel the sun's rays piercing my skin, probably because we were over 2,000 meters above sea level.

We walked through the gate to the main house where Stephanie and her family live. On the way, Samuel, Stephanie's husband, and Zoë and Cheyenne's father, appeared, bare-chested and shaggy-haired. It wasn't the first time I'd seen his face, as his picture had appeared prominently in the magazine "México Desconocido", where I'd learned about the ranch. The chilled-out American dude I had seen in the magazine with his hair tied back looking so at peace with the world, now sported gray hair that was all over the place, like a lion's mane, as well as crow feet wrinkles decorating his eyes. Importantly though, he came across as being very friendly. He is an American, so the real pronunciation should be just "Samuel", but his wife Stephanie calls him with the accent on the "e" in Samuel, like in Spanish.

Next, a young man with perfect blondish hair, wearing sunglasses, sits with his legs thrown out on the grass and his body propped up behind him. His plain black t-shirt and brown trousers seem to have been chosen so the dirt from his hard days of toil would blend in with the color scheme.

"Nice to meet you. I'm David from San Francisco."

He is a white, curly-haired, slightly portly young man. He has brown eyes and looks to be in his mid-thirties. Spookily for me, his smile made me think of when I was a shy student back in Japan and would avoid other guys who had the very same beam on their faces. But I later found out that this was a terrible prejudice on my part, and that he was a serious and dedicated engineer. An extremely pleasant fellow.

On the vast green lawn in front of the main house, there is a table for six made of logs. A brown-skinned woman who was kneading clay to make what looks like pottery smiled at me. I couldn't shake her hand in greeting because of the sticky clay, but she told me her name was Lavanya from Sri Lanka, who at present was living in San Francisco. She looked about the same age as David. I was puzzled when she started to speak in native-sounding American English. Her big eyes were attached to an exotic South Asian face. David and Lavanya were traveling together as "friends"staying in the same room in the guesthouses. There was no whisper of love between them during my stay, so I guessed they were sharing a room as "friends".

David was born in Russia, but his whole family moved to the USA when he was ten years old. So he is Russian-American. Lavanya is more Sri Lankan-American as she has worked for more than ten years in San Francisco where she moved with her family from her country of origin. My image of a typical Sri Lankan is one of the saris, gold bangles, and a red bindi in the middle of the forehead. But Lavanya had short hair and wore jeans and trainers. The mystery couple are in fact both single. I was told later that 90% of the guests at the Evergreen Ranch are foreigners, especially from Europe, who come here to learn the art of horsemanship, which involves communicating with the horses, and to experience country life. Perhaps the fact that French and English are spoken here is one of the reasons that attract westerners to such a remote place. And every once in a while, a Japanese person like me wanders in to add the international fusion of the place.

Stephanie led me into the main house, where there was a long wooden table in the middle of the room, which could seat about ten people if required. It was a “dining table”, an “office desk”, a “reception counter” and a “children’s study desk”. In a normal hotel, this would be just the reception. I had already rented a room to sleep in for 700 pesos (420 yen) and had previously paid for my meals and accommodation via net banking in advance. We had already exchanged emails back and forth eight times, but this was my first actual encounter with this multinational family. I felt welcome and at home.

“It’s cold, so bring a jumper”, “Do you eat meat or fish?” It was a friendly and pleasant exchange as if they were welcoming a friend or relative who was coming from far away after a long absence. After being told about the cheapest way to get around, I ended up arriving at the ranch for 280 pesos (1,700 yen) instead of taking a taxi directly from the airport for 1,000 pesos (6,000 yen), although it took longer.

Stephanie takes on the role of a hostess in a Japanese guest house. When guests arrive, she shows them where they will be staying, prepares their meals, handles the bills, and takes reservations. She also makes everyone feel part of her family, meaning that every guest who has booked a room with meals included will have a meal with the family.

By the way, the reason why the French woman is in the interior of Chiapas is that she traveled all over Mexico and liked this place the best, so she settled here. French life was nice, but she had always loved being surrounded by nature, so the peaceful life in the village of San Isidro Chichihuistan as well as the excitement of running the ranch was a good fit. She first met Samuel, an American, at another ranch in Mexico and for the last seven years, they have been running the Evergreen Ranch and receiving like-minded guests.

Samuel, on the other hand, had been working with horses in the USA for many years before coming to Mexico. He has worked with horses on farms and trained racehorses in various places. For thirteen years he traveled from place to place in Mexico. It was during this time that Stephanie arrived as a student at a ranch where he was giving classes for horse riding. Since then they have been living together. Samuel is responsible for the general care of the ranch and is also the instructor for the guests' riding activities. He also takes care of all the animals and feeds them on the 37 hectares of land. The hectares may not sound like much, but it is the size of eight Tokyo Domes.

There are four members in the family, two daughters aged 14 and 16, and the co-owner couple. But there are fourteen horses, five dogs and five cats, four sheep, a cow, maybe eight chickens, and a turkey. All of them have glossy coats and feathers, and you can tell at a glance that they are well-fed. If you consider all of them to be one then, they are quite a big family.

As I was listening to Stephanie's orientation about the place nodding my head in agreement, the fourteen-year-old Cheyenne kept looking at the large glass window behind me. She looked at her reflection in the window, tweaking her fringe and changing the angle of her face, looking pleased with herself. Does she have an admirer visiting the ranch and is too occupied with that, so she's not engaging in conversation at all, what's with that? I said to myself. But Stephanie told me that she had just cut her fringe for the first time in her life, just before I met her in Betania. I had seen a picture of her in a magazine and she looked much younger than she does now, with a very different expression. Of course, a woman's hair is her life, so she was curious to see how she looked after the change. Mom Stephanie told me secretly that she was quite pleased because she looked more mature than she thought she did. Cheyenne's elder sister, Zoë, had the same reaction when she cut her fringe for the first time according to Stephanie.

By the way, the eldest daughter, Zoë, who was 16 years old, was staying with her grandmother from France (Stephanie's mother) in the town of San Cristobal, the biggest tourist town around here, which many travelers enjoy visiting. Grandma, who is from Lyon, doesn't like living in the country, so she keeps her main accommodation in San Cristobal and only comes to the Evergreen Ranch to see her family just during Christmas. That's why I won't see Zoë and her grandmother for two days till Christmas Eve. I was looking forward to it.

The horses of the Evergreen Ranch.

-08-

Barn-Style Hut

Stephanie took me to the barn-like hut where I would be staying. It's a simple wooden hut about a hundred meters from the main house, across the lawn. The entrance leads to a common kitchen, with doors to the rooms on either side. I was taken to the wooden barn room on the right. In contrast to the concrete kitchen, the room is small with the scent of wood.

"This is your room. You can use any of the beds."

She showed me a queen size bed that was folded up on the wall vertically. The room also had bunk beds. With this pop-up bed, the room can accommodate up to four people. So she asked me if I wanted to book one bed or the whole room. But the idea of sharing such a small room with other travelers from different countries was still a bit much for me, a formerly shy person. I was afraid that I could snore or talk in my sleep and such close quarters would upset or freak out any poor unfortunate that shared with me.

The room opposite mine, to the left of the shared kitchen, is sometimes used by guests but is more for volunteers who come to help with carpentry work. It has bunk beds on either side and can sleep up to four people. This barn-like hut was built by Samuel himself and has a handmade feel to it. I was then shown to the toilets and showers at the back of the hut. The bare bark shower room was barely big enough for one person, but with a small changing room next to it, it was enough to freshen up. If you use it during the day, the boiler tank is heated up in the sunshine, giving you just the right amount of hot water without having to light a fire. Then, the wood is stoked after dark and the hot water is ready. Stephanie and Samuel are the ones who burn the wood. It's the ultimate solar power system, with hot water produced by the heat of the sun during the day. Indeed, with the sunlight beating down on this cylindrical boiler so intensely it is no surprise the water produced is so hot.

Then the toilet. When the wooden door was pulled forward, a wooden lid with a handle, painted emerald green, was placed on the toilet bowl. When you lifted it, there was a hole about a meter deep, into which both number ones and twos fell. Naturally, there was no flushing.

"You can pee here, but you don't have to do it in the toilet. You can do it anywhere on the ranch if you want. And after you've unleashed hell, there's one thing I'd like you to do. Please put the ashes in this bucket on top."

The wood burnt for hot water is turned into ashes after bathing, which is used for deodorization and disinfection, and the poo mixed with the ashes is finally returned to the soil. The "environmentally friendly recycling society" that is so much in demand around the world has been beautifully realized at this nature-inspired oasis.

"I'll call you when lunch is ready, which will be about half-past three. In the meantime, take a walk, read a book, or just rest. You can go anywhere on the ranch, walk around and get some fresh air. But there is only one rule that you must obey."

Stephanie said as she draped the hammock between the trees so that I could rest.

"When you go in and out of a fenced area, please make sure that you put the doorstop on to prevent the animals from escaping. You can't leave it open. Other than that, you can do whatever you like."

After telling me this, she went back to the main house to prepare a meal. The land looked huge. Wooden fences divided the space and the animals were arranged accordingly. The horses, in particular, are told to stay here and eat their food or to go over there and accompany the guests on their rides. It's like they know what they need to do now by where they are. Even so, animals other than horses and sheep, such as dogs, cats, and chickens, are so small that they can slip through any fence.

I thought I'd lie down, relax on the hammock behind the hut and read the novel I had brought with me. And for five whole minutes, I did. But the sky is so wide and the winter highlands air was so chilly that I decided against it. All I could see was an ax, a pile of firewood, two Toyota pick-up trucks with flat tires, and a green tractor. Restless to begin with, I decided to take a wander around the ranch until lunch. The intensive green grass is covered with a mixture of animal droppings, large and small. All this goes back into the ground as fertilizer, so it doesn't seem dirty at all. Unlike the dung lying on the concrete in the city, left by pathetic dog owners, it feels precious even. And it doesn't smell. All the farms I know with cows and horses have a strong smell of dung, but here I don't have to worry about that. Maybe it's because the land is so vast and the density of animals is so low.

All the animals have unique characteristics that keep you entertained. When the dogs see someone, they rush up to them, looking up at them, hoping to have their bellies rubbed. As I didn't want to get my hands dirty before lunch, I tried not to touch them, so they looked at me as if to say, "We're getting used to people so much, but you don't want to play with us, that makes us feel lonesome". When one of the dogs gives up and disappears, one of the other dogs lays on his back and exposes his belly for me to play with. Another one rubs his back against my leg. Cats, on the other hand, would come up to me and meow, but as soon as they knew that I would not fall for their feline charms, they left me alone to walk around freely, then the next thing I know, they are lazing on the grass with their eyes closed, content with the world. If I don't make a fuss of them, they leave me alone and just walk around at their will. A cat's selfishness is easy to understand, while at the same time they look so graceful.

Just as I was thinking this, a group of chickens were clamoring in front of me, completely ignoring the fence division, pecking at the ground, and being chased by dogs as they went. For some reason, a turkey with a slightly tearful look on its face lags behind the group. He must think he is a chicken. A large rooster with a straight back, or rather a straight neck, and a keen eye is always at the center of the flock, headed by him and accompanied by this sad-looking turkey as his faithful henchman. The sorrowful-looking turkey is only a little larger than the chickens and has a slightly different call. This sad fellow will flock with whoever feels pity for him. Together, this feather-clad militia-trained posse is a formidable force, ready to fight back against a dog or cat if they are chased as a group rather than if they are alone.

It's only a small part of the large estate. After a short walk, I was unpacking in my room when Stephanie came to tell me that lunch was ready.

This small room can accommodate up to four people.

-09-

Blackboard and Chalk

There are only two huts at the Evergreen Ranch for guests to stay in. Apart from the barn-style hut where I stay, there is "The Cottage", where Lavanya and David are camped. This is a fine guest house with a fireplace. This means that Lavanya and David are the lucky ones, due to the fact they will be nice and warm when the coldness of the mountain air hits home. They usually cook for themselves in their room, so I was the only one to share a meal with the owners' family. It's like a homestay because I'm sitting at the table with Stephanie, horseman Samuel, and their daughter Cheyenne. I chose my staples from Stephanie's homemade crepes, tortillas (handmade in the village), and wholemeal hard bread, and ate them with finely chopped fruit, freshly cooked vegetables, and a bean dish called "Frijoles" in Spanish. They even go to the trouble of cooking chicken or pork for me. They seem to be 'almost' vegetarians, and they've bought meat and fish for me, as I'd requested in advance. "If you want to add meat to your meal, it's 50 pesos (300 yen) extra," they said in the email, because they make one extra dish for the guests, in addition to the family meal.

Having eaten very little all morning, I tucked into a warm, soft tortilla with a mild homemade chili sauce, grilled onions and chicken simply seasoned with salt, then rolled it up. The ingredients are all locally sourced.

As I enjoy the meal and learn more about the village and the family, I realize that their lives are quite simple. They provide accommodation for guests from all over the world and teach horse riding. They sometimes take their horses on tours of the mountains and offer food and wine on request for an extra charge. They feed and nurture the animals on the ranch and keep the vast property in as natural a state as possible. Samuel, the father, and the husband who was a carpenter in addition to working with horses in the US, so he knows how to repair and build houses.

The village of San Isidro Chichihuistan has a population of around 270. The houses and small churches made of wood and bricks are scattered along the flat road and the slope leading up to the mountain. The majority of the inhabitants are indigenous Mayans, who speak Spanish in addition to their native language, Tzotzil (there are more than sixty indigenous languages in Mexico). In this context, a ranch run by a foreign family seems quite different and special in the village. The family's love of nature and their sincere character probably won them over. From time to time, local children and men would come to the property to assist their American and French friends in any way they can around the ranch. They call Samuel "Don Samuel" as a term of endearment. "Don" is a traditional Mexican term for a man who is an elder. It is used to show respect. In Japan, the word "Okina" was used frequently in ancient times in the same way as, 'Don'. Today though it is not so common to hear this in my home country. In this small village, there is a clear sense of solidarity as friends living together in a beautiful environment. The villagers also enjoy the small economic benefits that come from the ranch, as they are paid for helping out with carpentry work, such as renovating the roof. This is how they have managed to stay firmly rooted in the land and run the Evergreen Ranch for seven years now.

The eldest daughter, Zoë, has recently started high school, but until then both Zoë and her sister Cheyenne have been educated completely at home. Math, history, literature, geography, how to write - everything. I knew that one of my old university friends, a German lady, had educated her kids at home. Cheyenne, however, was the first person I had met who had been brought up in this way.

"Zoë insisted on going to school, so I sent her, but I still don't think she needs it," Stephanie said.

Being here at the ranch reminds me that the path that most Japanese take for granted - graduating from school and getting a job at a company - is just one of an infinite number of options. The truth is that it would take a lot of determination for a person like me, who has lived in a city immersed in the school culture for a long time, to educate my children all by myself. As a parent of children of the same ages as Stephanie's, I am not at all sure that I would be able to answer all the simple questions my children would have and teach them in the same way they learn in traditional education.

There was a blackboard on the outside wall of the main house. It was about the size of my outstretched arms. There were numbers and letters written on it with chalk.

"Is this what you used to teach your children to study?"

I asked Stephanie.

"Yes, we used to use it a lot when they were little. But we don't use it much anymore."

It seems that this blackboard and the big table in the main house are the study places for Zoë and Cheyenne.

The chicken boss and the sheep.

Chapter Three

The Horse that Laughs in the Moonlight

-10-

Equitation

I had eaten all of the delicious food I had been served along with a glass of Spanish red wine that complemented the dish perfectly when I looked up and noticed the dynamic San Francisco duo of Lavanya and David sitting and looking bored outside the main house. The reason being was that they had horses to ride and were eager to start.

"They're waiting for you," said my gracious host, Samuel.

"Be ready to start riding as soon as you feel fit."

The main attraction of this ranch is horse riding. Of course, any hotel in the touristic town of San Cristobal will be able to arrange a horse ride in the immediate vicinity. But the reason why so many westerners come here is that it is a rare place where you can learn how to communicate with a horse in an authentic way. It's called Equitation. As Samuel is the only teacher, any guest interested in taking part, will be taken under his wing.

After realizing I was holding up the post-lunch entertainment, I made haste to my room, filled up a bottle of water, applied sunscreen to my face and arms, and rushed outside to join David and Lavanya. I shoved the bottle in my backpack because my angel doctor with her purring tone had told me to drink lots of water while taking the medicine she had prescribed for my swollen throat. Preferably two or three liters a day. Plenty of sunscreen is required, due to the sun being strong during the day on the highland. By this time David and Lavanya were inching to get started and were waiting with Samuel on the grass for my arrival.

The horses have a variety of places to reside here on the ranch. But most of the time they stay in their enclosures. In the enclosure where each horse is kept, there is a colorful, hand-painted name tag. But the horses, which of course can't read, don't care where they call home, and casually wander into the area designated for another nag. So even though all fourteen horses had names like "Shiraz" and "Zeus", I could barely remember which one was which. Next to the elegant four-legged beast's housing project, a feeding shed can be found. There is a feed box in the shed at chest height so that the horses can eat without having to lower their heads to the ground. Comfort at its finest.

The beginning of the dressage class is surprisingly unassuming, starting in a small storeroom beside the feeding stable. Inside there is a large sack full of corn kernels. The dry kernels were the same orange color as the corn I had eaten earlier in San Cristobal. Samuel turned to us and explained the process of soaking the kernels in a solution of lime. The maize had been dipped into a small white bucket of water beforehand making them softer than dry grain. He then began to spread the moist grain on the ground. The three of us imitated him, grabbing the corn from a mini tub he had given us and sprinkling it onto the earth below. Immediately, a group of hungry, noisy, chickens began to cluck and peck at the soil.

To my mind, Samuel wanted to demonstrate to us country life neophytes how the grain born from the earth is given to the chickens and the droppings they so frequently produce make the land fertile. "Nothing is wasted," he reiterated as he fed the chickens.

Next, we went to the tool shed. There are reins on the wall and seven black helmets on a shelf. They were riding helmets that protruded slightly at the brim. The three of us chose our reins and helmets respectively. My head was bigger than the other two, so there was only one helmet that would fit. At first, David took it, but then I had to ask David to swap it with me because my head didn't fit in the helmet I had. The bigger the head, the larger the brain. That's my motto. Also, I was the tallest out of the 3 of us. With my grand head and long legs, could I be destined to be the greatest horse rider the ranch had ever seen? Only time would tell.

Once out of the tool shed, the next step is the choice of the saddle for each rider. There are four main types of saddle, from the thick leather western style to the thin leather training saddles used for racing horses. The saddles were laid out on a waist-high log stand, and Samuel explained to us what each one was for. As I looked at the saddles, I noticed that what I had ridden in the tourist areas of Mexico was usually used for working in fields. And it seems that the saddles we will be using are mainly western.

After a briefing on the equipment, each of us was introduced to our partner horse for the day. My partner was a brown mare called "Neirida". David's significant other would be 'Ginger' and 'Pepsi' had been selected for Lavanya.

Each of us three eager students learned from Samuel how to attach a halter to the horse's head, which in Japanese is called "Toraku". First, the leather halter is looped over the nose, then over the back of the head. After this has been done correctly, the length has to be adjusted. The key is to apply it lightly and never tighten it. Fortunately, our horses are used to this routine and do not resist. Then, from a black plastic box on the grass, each of us picked up a brush with bristles as hard and similar to a needle point holder for flower arrangement. Brushing is an important time for communicating with the horse. Back in Japan, I used to have a Shiba Inu dog as a pet that I would brush when I was little, but of course, a horse has a much larger area to groom. While brushing my newly found friend, I was delighted to find Neirida's coat to be luscious and moist. Through this interaction, I knew that she was being well looked after during her time here.

Next on the agenda, I was taught how to lift the horse's heavy legs and remove mud and stones from its hooves with a key-shaped pick. I put my elbow on the horse's knee and let it bend while I gently lifted her leg, which required a lot of strength. Due to the weight of Lavanya's trusty steed, Samuel helped her with this process. Finally, as I looked upward, I found that the soles of my companion's feet were filled with mud and pebbles. I scraped out the debris with a pick as carefully as I could so as not to hurt her.

As I had ridden a horse at a tourist attraction before, I thought I could ride on my own, because I imagined I knew a bit about horses. However, as Samuel explained to me about the horses that I, as well as my companions, were bonding with, I soon realized that there were many things I didn't know about them. For example, I learned for the first time that there is soft meat hidden inside the hoof, like a dog's or cat's paw. Also, under Samuel's guidance, it was the first time that I had spoken to a horse in Japanese. What is more, I had never seen the look of comfort on a horse's face that I had the joy of witnessing as I groomed it, until now.

I was wandering around her, from head to tail, brushing the flesh of her ample belly and firm chin when suddenly Neirida stepped on my foot. Her left hoof rested on the top of my foot without hesitation. I was shocked. According to Samuel, a horse weighs six hundred kilos, so by simple calculation, a quarter of that - one hundred and fifty kilos - would be on the top of my poor tootsie. But even if I tried to release my trampled foot, the horse would not easily raise her leg. She didn't even seem to be aware that she was stepping on my foot in the first place. Fortunately, I didn't get hurt as I was wearing tennis shoes with a slightly stiffened upper part of the shoe. Luckily for me, this extra protection softened the impact. Samuel, however, came up to me when he noticed that I had suddenly stopped brushing.

"Did you get trampled?"

Samuel said with a grin. When we first met, he spoke to me in broken Spanish, but by this time we were speaking exclusively in his native tongue, English.

"Don't get too close to the horse. Always touch the horse with your hand, and keep just far enough away that she doesn't step on you, but close enough to let her know you're here. If she still steps on your foot, you can lightly push her body with your hand and she will know to raise her leg."

I tried my best to get close to her, talking to Neirida and occasionally whispering gently in her ears, but it didn't seem that the closer physical distance between us aided the enhancement of our bond. Samuel also added a note of caution when walking around the horse's hindquarters.

"If you are afraid of being kicked and keep too far away from the horse, it can be dangerous. If you do get kicked, the horse's hind legs will go into overdrive. That's why you should always go around with your palm touching her back and legs to let her know where you are. If you are close enough to touch her, even if you are standing by her rear end, she will not let out a strong kick. The danger is when you're a little away from her that her hind leg extends when she kicks out."

It certainly seems that if I'm close enough, there's no distance for her to kick me even if I'm close to her rear end.

Finally, I was stepped on twice, but the second time I was not so startled, and I gently pushed the horse's belly with my hands and politely asked her to move her feet. As I carefully brushed Neirida, I had the feeling that she was controlling the situation, and not me. Till then, horses had been an animal that took me for rides, but they had never been something with which I felt a connection. But as I rubbed the brush across her cheekbones and under her chin, Nailida's eyes narrowed as if she was entranced. I thought she'd fallen asleep standing up. But sometimes I'd slack off for a while and she'd take hold of the cuff of my shirt and give it a strong tug. Not once, not twice, but several times. Each time I would look back at Neirida in surprise, she would deliberately turn away with an "I didn't do anything" look on her face. Samuel, who was watching her said, "An old horse like Neirida knows all about how to get you to do what she wants."

A grin appeared across his face. Unwittingly, I had become Neiridas' very own personal assistant.

The veteran mare Neirida.

-11-

Energy from the Sun

Once the horses were back in their dwelling, Samuel led us across the middle of the pasture, where we had to pass through several fences as we made our way deeper and deeper into the huge field. With some of them, you had to lift one of the wooden bars that ran across horizontally to pass to the other side, then bring it back down to its resting place. Other fences had a gated entrance that needed to be opened, then securely closed before we moved on to the next one. For our pleasure, there was nothing but picturesque greenery to be viewed.

"Inhale deeply and then exhale. Feel the energy of the earth."

The shaggy-headed Samuel looks and talks like a hippy, who happens to be middle-aged now. The three of us took off our shoes as he asked us to. We spread open our arms, stretched out our chests to the sun, and took a deep breath. Due to being a city dweller, it had been a while since I had been barefoot outside on grass, so it felt good to feel the cool, prickly tips of the grass on my feet.

"We require the sun's energy to live. So do plants and animals."

He urged us to look towards the sun. Samuel takes great pride in talking to his students about the bountiful nature to be found in that vast field. In the clear air of the Chiapas highlands, there is nothing to block the sun. In addition, the sky is decorated in deep blue with clouds few and far between. Samuel begins to stare at the sun while instructing us not to protect our eyes with our hands due to the glare.

"You'll get used to looking directly at the sun with your naked eyes. Try it."

No matter how much I tried, my eyes just hurt. Neither I understood the benefits of doing so, and I stopped immediately, sorry to say because it seemed to be damaging my eyes.

"The sun gives us many things. And water. However, we can't live on water and light alone, but the benefits are immeasurable. You should say 'thank you' every time you drink water."

As he tells us in such an intense and serious way, gradually a strange feeling comes to my mind that people should also be able to live by photosynthesis. Samuel believes that it would be best if we didn't rely on anything artificial. The meadow is surrounded by a forest that has from one side of it a single thick wire crossing far above the ranch and then disappears into the forest on the other side.

"It's a shame about these wires." Samuel murmured to no one in particular.

On the way back to the stables after this session of "appreciating nature and living on sun and water", Lavanya, the Sri Lankan-American, asked me how I knew about the ranch.

"I read about it in a magazine and it looked like a really interesting place, but I couldn't decide to come here with my family. So I decided to come here over the holidays when I could travel alone."

That's how I ended up at this ranch. There must be some kind of common orientation for us to come to this remote place.

"I was told by people I knew and friends I met on my travels that the ranch was very attractive. When I heard about it, I just had to come."

She told me that she was in the middle of a year-long trip around Latin America after quitting her job. Lavanya now has a lot of time on her hands, so even though she knew it was not easy to get to, she was more than happy to make this little detour.

That afternoon, in a session that lasted about two hours, we were taught how to get on a horse only for a short while. But we didn't get to "ride" the horses. There is a lot more to learn before that. How to deal with nature on the ranch, for example. Sitting on the grass around Samuel under a blue sky, we had an introductory session until it started to get a bit chilly as the sunset.

Samuel is a quiet man who is always on the move, tending to the ranch, but when he starts talking about horses and nature he suddenly becomes very talkative. He has an infectious energy and a great sense of humor. Before we know it, we are drawn in by his energy and become his disciples. Incidentally, Samuel seemed to have a habit of inventing nicknames. I wondered if he was having trouble remembering people's names, but then I thought about the names of the fourteen horses that he knew so well. Taking this into consideration, he might not be interested in remembering the names of tourists who come and go every day. David, a Russian-American, was named "Einstein". I think it's because of his curly, bushy hair, but actually, Samuel has shaggy, Einstein-esque hair.

"I think you're more like Einstein than I am."

David put up a small fight, but there was no way he was winning this conflict about nicknames. It seems that David is called Einstein not because he looks like him, but only because it is easy to remember. In contrast, the girls are never given nicknames. Samuel, a gentleman who grew up in the US, calls the boys by their nicknames, but never the girls. According to his wife Stephanie, he was very popular with the ladies when he was young, and this may be one of the reasons why. He also worked as an actor in Hollywood.

"I'm sure he had a lot of girlfriends while he was moving from one place to another in Mexico before he met me. But you'll have to ask him about that when I'm not around."

I remember Stephanie saying jokingly with a wink.

And as for me, Samuel has named me "Synergy". This is easy to understand because my name is "Shinji" and it sounds similar. I wish he'd just pronounce it as "Shinji", but it's more convenient for him to translate it so that it's a little easier to remember. Over the next three days, my name had morphed from the classic original Shinji, to "Shiniji" with the extra 'i' without realizing when.

Samuel explains how to communicate with a horse.

-12-

The Horse that Laughs in the Moonlit Night

On the way back to my room after the first day's activities, I told Stephanie that I wanted to take a shower before dark, so she put some wood in the boiler to heat some water. The shower room was only big enough for one person to fit in, but in the chilly weather, it was perfect to keep the heat in. The water exiting the shower head was hot and sprayed out in a fine, strong mist. Soon there was so much steam within the petit shower room that it felt like a sauna. The wooden shower room was quite simple in the way it had been made, with only a single wooden door separating it from the changing room, which is covered from head height to just below the knees. So the cold air from outside enters without an invitation from above and below. I rinsed myself off post-haste and moseyed into my room in shorts, a T-shirt, and flip-flops, with a bath towel over my head. Fashionista alert!!!

I put on a pair of jeans and a fresh shirt and finally settled down on my bed in my room. It was a relief after all the traveling to arrive here, to have taken a shower, and enjoy some downtime by myself. I checked the screen of my mobile phone through habit. The WiFi in the main house doesn't reach this far, so of course, there's no signal on the phone.

"Desconectarse de todo (Disconnect from all)."

Stephanie's words sprang to mind describing the way how to enjoy the Evergreen Ranch.

Soaked in the sunshine and refreshed by a hot shower, I was feeling pleasantly tired and a little uplifted.

At dusk, I went out to the main house again. I just wanted to talk to someone. From the first day I met Stephanie and Samuel and their second daughter, I felt welcome and enjoyed walking around the large ranch with David and Lavanya of "the horse-riding beginners' club". This is very different from the relationship between guests at a beach resort, where there is no feeling of solidarity. Nobody seems to wish to connect. After a while, I managed to meet David and Lavanya on the way. They showed me the supreme hut where they were staying. "The Cottage" was a lot more solid and spacious than my barn-like hut. As you enter the front door, there is a fireplace to the left, where you can light a fire with wood from the ranch. At the back of the room was a private kitchen, where the two self-catering guests had laid out several small bottles containing various spices.

In a short while, Samuel arrived with some wood and used a match to light it. Slowly the flames spread through the wood, helping to create a crackling sound, and the smoke was sucked up into the chimney. On the highlands of Chiapas, where the sun had tucked itself in for the night, it was getting chilly. We three novice horsemen gathered around the fireplace, almost hypnotized by the dancing flames, and listened to Samuel's quiet ramblings about the fire. It was indeed a delightful, cozy fire that he had made.

Christmas was just around the corner, but surprisingly there was no festive atmosphere in the village. The only thing I was fed up with in this village was the pastor's loud microphone he joyously used around 6 pm. There was no hiding place from this torture, as it was so loud we were forced to listen to it while I was having dinner with Samuel and Stephanie in the main house. The vicar seems to be intoxicated by his own words, but truthfully the content is very simple.

"Don't drink too much, boys."

"Don't touch any other girl but your wife after you marry her, boys."

He preaches endlessly and cries out repeatedly, interspersing stories from the Bible. It may be that in the villages around here, there are often incidents of drunken men misbehaving with girls.

"He put it on speaker and made it too loud. This is brainwashing, isn't it? "

Samuel doesn't like the way the missionaries use modern devices like microphones and speakers to amplify the sound, rather allowing the content of the story to be heard naturally.

But all this noise and over long masses suddenly quieten down just before 8 pm. I enjoyed a colorful vegetable dinner, chatting with Stephanie, Samuel, and Cheyenne. I left the main house after confirming breakfast time for the next day. The savior from darkness on the ranch at night is from the yellow lights leaking out from the main and guest houses, as well as the stunningly bright moonlight. The air is dry and unpolluted, so I can make out Orion and countless stars, even though I don't know much about constellations at all. Having finished my meal, I crossed the grassy field to return to my hut, pausing for a few minutes to admire the bright night sky and the faint light leaking through the windows of the main house.

There is no heating in my barn-like hut, which is made of boards, so it is cold in there. It's a stark contrast to David's hut with the fireplace. I decided to gather all the blankets from the bunk beds, which were folded up. In total, I collected four. I end up sleeping on the bottom bunk. As soon as I crawled under the newly hunted blankets, my body was indeed warm, but my face was so cold that it made my skin crawl. So I pulled one of them up to my nose leaving my eyes exposed, and tried to breathe slowly so that my warm breath wouldn't escape.

When I turn off the light, I can see through the small window the yellow light from the main house where I spent time with the family. Between the hut and the main house, there is a handmade volleyball net made of twine. Outside is bright from the natural light of the stars and the moon. As soon as the imitation lights are turned off, it becomes darker in my wooden sanctuary. This is what I'm looking for: a place without artificiality, without the internet and all the conveniences of electronics, just looking up at the sky, breathing in and breathing out. This simple way of spending time is a luxury. The Evergreen Ranch receives requests from all over the world to book one of the only two huts in the world that offer this feeling.

By the way, I'm embarrassed to say that on my first night in my hut, I woke up in the middle of the night, due to a call of nature. I needed to pee. I was told by the doctor to drink a lot of water because I had started to catch a cold, so, as a good patient, I just kept on drinking. It's bright outside by the light of the moon, so any other form of illumination is not required, even at midnight. On the contrary, it is darker in the enclosed shower room and toilet. So I took advantage of Stephanie's generous offer to take a tinkle wherever I found a spot outside that appealed. For sure, I could have done it in the toilet, but it would have been a shame to be born a man and have to do it in a small, dark space when such a vast area was on offer. I also felt that spending a penny in the toilet would be unhygienic, as it would concentrate the filth there.

The experience turned out to be so delightful. I tried to do my business outside in the daytime, however, the plains were so spectacular I couldn't bring myself to forever blemish them with my liquid discharge. Additionally, I couldn't find a patch of grass that would cover me completely from the waist down. With this in mind, I decided that I didn't want to be the free entertainment for the day and refrained from doing so, thinking that it would be quite awkward for all concerned if I came eye to eye with someone whilst in the act.

That night, I took an open-air leak. Despite the feeling of freedom, I was more worried about what would happen if someone saw me. And, finally, someone was watching me. Right next to the cluster of grass, which I had chosen after some hesitation, there was a stable, which I hadn't paid much attention to during the day and I felt the presence of a creature. Before my very eyes, an insomniatic horse was peeking over the stable gate.

I said, "I'm sorry," as I went about my business, and the brown horse paced back and forth in the shed, occasionally resting his chin on the fence, looking pleased with himself. It was a lonely night for him, isolated and alone, when "a human" suddenly appeared. He thought that the human with the oversized cranium looked harmless enough. Then he started to pee. "Oh well, I don't mind." Lit up by the moonlight, the four-legged chap had such a mischievous look on his face as if he was about to laugh. As I hadn't seen him during the daytime session, maybe he was a young horse who hadn't yet been allowed to make his debut in the dressage school. I looked up at the sky and saw the exquisite moon shining much brighter than the city's night lights.

Moonlight and the main house.

-13-

The Relationship Between Hooves and Dogs

The next morning I woke up with a spring in my step. The sore throat was almost gone, thanks to the medicine. My wonderful softly spoken doctor advised me to drink plenty of water, so I carried a bottle with me all the time and drank during the equestrian activities.

I took off my pajamas, put on a pair of jeans, a t-shirt, and a heavy sweatshirt, left the hut, and washed my face in the sink outside the shower room. The water was early morning, countryside cold, and performed better than my usual alarm clock, waking me up instantly. I put my trusty water bottle and camera in my backpack and left the room to go to the main house where Stephanie and her family reside. There is always a set of chairs and a table for six outside the main house. The dogs lie on the table like they own the place. To the left of the entrance, there was a long, narrow wooden bench, on which the cats would perch, hoping to get in at any opportunity. I open the door to the main house and Stephanie greets me, careful not to let any of the cats around my feet slip inside. She's smiling as ever.

"Did you sleep well? Were you cold?"

"At first, but later it was fine", I said honestly.

"I slept with all the blankets in the room covering my nose because my face was so cold. Why isn't there a pane of glass in the window frame in the kitchen next to that room?"

Stephanie giggled when she heard this.

"You'll have to ask Samuel about that. He hasn't put it in yet, but I'm sure he will one day." I thought to myself, I hoped that day would be today because the coldness of the room is so intense.

"By the way, what would you like for breakfast? We serve fruit and yogurt, but you can also have wholemeal bread with tomatoes, onions, and eggs, or you can have crepes. A neighbor from the village has prepared tortillas for all of us to enjoy."

The French proprietress served a breakfast that was mainly fruit and vegetables, with a focus on making the most of the flavors of the ingredients. But it's not all French. They also serve frijoles, which are cooked beans and are an essential part of Mexican cuisine. I asked for a crepe that morning, preferably something I hadn't eaten before. The crepes are not sweetened with sugar, but rather have a slightly salty taste, although they have the same chunky texture that is so well-known in Japan. The classic crepe in Japan is simply rolled up and eaten with chocolate or jam. But here on the ranch it is served with a vegetable or bean filling. Stephanie said "OK" and in no time at all she had the dough baked in a pan and placed in front of me. I put tomatoes and onions on top of it, then chicken and frijoles joined the party. It was moister and more tender than I had imagined it would be, and I loved every bite.

Before I knew it, Stephanie had made me some coffee. The beans were local, from San Cristobal, and it looked like they had been ground in a coffee mill that very morning. I'm not a coffee expert by any means, but I've heard that the coffee from Chiapas is characterized by its high acidity. However, the freshly brewed coffee had a deep and fragrant aroma rather than acidity, which made me sigh with glee as I drank it.

Including myself, there were five of us in the dressage session that day. In addition to Lavanya and David from San Francisco, who had been with me since day one, a young Swedish couple joined us on a day trip.

"Shinji, all the members speak English very fluently, so if you don't understand something, stop the conversation and ask them, don't be shy." When I was leaving the table, Stephanie reminded me so. She is possibly the same age as me, maybe a little younger, but she advised me as if she was my mother. I said "OK, thanks" and joined the group.

As Stephanie had told us on the first day, the reputation of the ranch was spreading quickly amongst the Western travelers. The Swedish man who joined us that day was promptly nicknamed "Axel" by Samuel. The blond, shoulder-length hair surely reminded him of Guns N' Roses' vocalist Axel Rose. Maybe shorter and a little less wild than the original rocker, but still similar, I could say. The diminutive Swedish "Axel" always wore a black ten-gallon hat with a brim. His profession is a painter and decorator, but he has had three months off in a row and is on his way from Mexico to Guatemala. A quarter of the year is spent on holiday, which is enviable as even the summer holidays at primary school in Japan are only a month long, but at the same time, it made me worry about how hard it would be to get back into the job after the holidays are over. His girlfriend Anna, a beautiful Scandinavian blonde, didn't receive any nickname from Samuel of course because she is a member of the fairer species. They make a cute couple.

Scooby the dog and his friends are lounging in the sun on a table.

As these two newcomers—well, I had only arrived the day before—hadn't yet experienced the 'introduction to nature', Master Samuel started with a "chicken session" where we roughly scattered corn on the ground. The beaks of the chickens immediately followed as they pecked at the ground, searching for a tasty morsel, all the while making a scandalous noise, and we listened to Samuel's explanation of how food circulates in nature.

Each student then slowly led his or her partner out of the stable and into the middle of the pasture. Whenever you take a horse out of the enclosure, you have to go first and then lead the horse out. If you don't, you and your horse could bump into the fence surrounding the enclosure and get injured. True to Samuel's word, we tied the reins to a series of wooden poles in the middle of the meadow. Samuel's explanation of how to correctly attach the leather halter around the horse's head and secure the saddle on its back was as detailed and passionate as ever that day.

"Speak softly to the horses. It doesn't matter whether you are talking in Japanese, English, or Swedish, the horses can sense what you are thinking by the tone of your voice. This is true. So the most important thing is to talk to them in a respectful tone to build trust."

As he said this, Samuel took it in turns to help us, his pupils, with the brushing of the hair and cleaning of the soles. It still takes a lot of strength to bend the knee joint and pick out the dirt and pebbles from the horse's sole.

That day, by the way, I realized that a horse's "hoof" is the equivalent of a human being's "nail". Samuel took a sickle-like tool and sliced off a piece of hoof about an inch thick. The sliced piece of the white hoof was not on the same scale as a human trimming the top of a nail off with a nail clipper. The hoof in question was a little bigger than my palm, and looking at it, I thought it must be very painful as if the bone was being cut out. At that same moment, the impressive slice of hoof fell to the ground where two dogs were patiently waiting for it. They started gobbling it up as if they were competing with each other over a prime steak.

"It's their favorite food," Samuel said as if it were nothing special.

The day continued with the same routine as yesterday, brushing and otherwise communicating with the horses in one way or another. I rub the horse all over with a stiff bristle brush and the look in her eyes conveys nothing but pleasure. When I stroke her belly with my left hand, which is not holding the brush, my fingers sometimes touch a small protuberance. I ask Samuel if it's something like a wart, and he replies that it's a tick. The vampires that nest on these horses are fat and round. To remove them, you don't need to use much force. But we must not throw them on the ground.

"They are very dangerous," he said. "If you don't stamp them out completely, they will just hang around in the grass and suck on another horse's blood. They don't have favorites. So if you find one, remember what I told you. Don't throw it on the ground, put it in a bucket or there will be trouble later."

Samuel then peeled the tick off the horse's belly and dropped it into the tin bucket in his other hand.

In the second half of the introduction, we walk along the same route as yesterday to a meadow away from the main house. We walk for about five minutes, and at this time we have a chance to communicate with each other. It was during this walk that I had talked to Lavanya the day before. Today I was walking close to Anna, Axel's girlfriend, and I asked her if she had ever ridden a horse.

"I've ridden horses in Sweden, but only as a child, with someone pulling the reins for me to guide the horse around the park. It's not easy to find a place that teaches you like this."

She and I are not very different in that although we have both ridden horses, we don't know much about them.

The cats are outside the main house, always waiting for the right moment to sneak inside.

-14-

The Temperature of Mud

When we reached the middle of the meadow, Samuel asked the five of us to sit down in a circle. He had taken hold of a curious dog and was patting it on the neck. We listened to a series of explanations about the importance of water and how the sun's rays help plants to photosynthesize, which in turn are eaten by animals to sustain the cycle of life. Then, barefoot, looking at the sun, we opened our legs shoulder-width apart and let the air rush into our lungs. No one complains saying "I'm here to ride a horse, so let me ride a horse". Perhaps this is the kind of action that gives tourists a sense of spiritual satisfaction. I am one of them. When Samuel, with his lion's mane of gray hair, passes on his cycle of life knowledge we can only be convinced by his quiet, confident delivery.

But the day didn't end there.

"When you ride a horse, it is very important for you to shift and adjust your weight flexibly. Your weight doesn't seem so heavy to him but actually, it's very hard for the horse to carry you."

Upon saying this, Samuel imitated riding a horse as if he were taking the reins and started towards a small bog at the side of the field. The bog seemed to have a little water in it, but it was more or less mud. In the middle of the bog, which was divided into two parts, there was a narrow path with four brown horses eating weeds in it.

"Ideally, the person on top should have a picture in his mind of the direction to go, and the horse should follow it. But when the horse is stepping on the ground, we don't know how many stones are there or how thick the grass is. Of course, if the horse walks through the mud as we have here, we can't feel what a burden it is for him."

Telling us so, Samuel began to plunge his feet into the mud. He pulled his trousers up to his knees and asked us to follow him barefoot. I was at the back of the line containing his five students going all the way into the mud, so I had no choice but to put my feet in. It was similar to the feeling I had in my childhood when I put my feet in the mud of a paddy rice field. This time, however, my feet sank deeper and deeper. It's not so much walking as it is pulling your feet out one after the other, trying to keep your balance and not sink into the depths. The mud reached mid-calf, and it was beyond just cool. Chilly, would be a better word to use to describe the temperature. It was funny because at first, I thought I didn't want to be covered in mud, but then I began to find the slipperiness pleasant.

"You see, a horse may look like it can walk through mud, but it is just like you and me right now, it is difficult to balance. So, the person on top has to be aware of this and shift his weight according to the movement and the direction you are going."

You should never ride a horse through mud unless you're a very advanced rider, and none of the five of us were experienced enough to do so. Speaking for me, I was more interested in the seriousness of the session than anything else. My four colleagues, like me, have probably never by choice been barefoot in mud in their adult lives, nor have they ever put their dirty feet into socks after getting out of the mud, having only lightly brushed it off with their hands. The two Swedes on a day trip would have taken a taxi back to San Cristobal, where they were staying, with their muddy feet. Samuel was unconcerned about this and was making a passionate speech to us on the lawn. All the while we—especially Anna from Sweden—were trying our best to get the mud off with our hands. Me, David, and Lavanya, who were staying at the ranch, could go back to our rooms to change our clothes and have a shower. But Axel and Anna, who had come for a day trip, would never have thought of needing to bring a spare pair of socks with them. And this is exactly the kind of experience they would speak to others about and propagate most funnily and pleasantly in San Francisco or Sweden.

We then walked slowly back to where several horses were tied up. A white mare called "Dutchess" chosen from all of them for us to practice on one by one was an excellent partner who was so patient with beginners. As we took turns in riding her, each of us straddled her back, climbing on using the open palms of a fellow student as a step, and those who had to assist in lifting others had to get down on one knee to support all the weight. I was the one who lifted David who seemed to be the heaviest and was impressed by how the horse handled the weight. We then took turns walking slowly around the track while talking to Dutchess.

But the horse for some reason doesn't listen to me very well. To start her walking, I signaled by clamping both heels onto the horse's belly. At the same time, I purse my lips and inhale sharply, making a so-called kissing noise. The orthodox method is to shout "walk" while shifting your weight slightly forward with your hips. Being Japanese, I felt a bit embarrassed to say "walk" in English, so I translated it into Japanese as "Ike(go)" or "Aruke (walk)", but the horse, who appeared to have never heard such a signal before in a non-Latin rooted idiom, just looked back at me with a puzzled look and blinked her eyes. "You told me she could understand any language", Samuel's words had stayed with me, but they seemed to be effective only when I was brushing her to express my affection.

I regained my composure, changed the signal back to "walk" and finally, Dutchess started to move forward. I was supposed to ride her slowly around the meadow, controlling the reins, but it didn't go so well. We stopped at a water trough on the way and she started to drink. At first, I tolerated her, thinking she was thirsty, but she never finished. It crossed my mind that maybe she was taking antibiotics. When she looked up a little to catch her breath, I pulled hard on the reins and tried to get her to lift her head, but she started drinking again. I didn't think she was listening to me at all. Seeing that I was stuck for so long, Samuel came to my rescue.

"You don't need to give her more time to drink water. She's had enough already."

Samuel gently touched the horse's belly with his hands and spoke softly to Dutchess, then with a firm yank on the reins, turned the horse to face the direction I wanted her to go. I remembered that when I had ridden horses at other tourist attractions, there had always been a horse owner or owner's child leading the way. In short, I didn't know how to get a horse to start without someone guiding me. Samuel led the way, and finally, Dutchess walked off again, looking rather annoyed. Maybe she had been drinking water not because she was thirsty, but just because she didn't want to walk around with me on her back.

Samuel with his disciples trudging through the mud.

Chapter Four

Mountains, Radio Waves and a Love Letter

-15-

Into the Deep Forest of Chiapas

After the morning session, it was time for lunch. All the novice riders went to the main house and were treated to a meal cooked by Stephanie. Samuel and Cheyenne were there too. We were served pork ribs on the bone, which was a delight to see, as I was very hungry after all the activities I had done. The mashed potato salad was served in a bowl in the middle of the table. Her dishes are always accompanied by finely chopped purple onions and small cubes of bright red tomatoes, so the colors are always vibrant and inviting. After the scrumptious lunch, we went outside and had a coffee on the wooden deck.

As we sat at the table, Samuel was smoking a cigarette as he stood. He began to talk about his adventures in Mexico, making theatrical gestures as he did so.

"Who's ever been bungee jumping?"

There was no one with any experience of this insane pastime, among us. All of us here are quite adventurous up to a point, I believe, but this activity of leaping from some high vantage point with nothing but a glorified elastic band to save your skin is a bridge too far.

"The first time I bungee jumped into the sea in Cancun, I was terrified."

Samuel usually comes across as a man with no fear, but as he told us his post-lunch stuntman tale, you could feel the tension of being on the verge of jumping into the abyss.

"I was standing on the platform ranting about whether I'm going to fly from here or not. Then the loving instructor gave me a little nudge and before I knew it, I was driving towards the surface. For a terrifying moment, the water was right there in front of me and then I was whipped upwards like a rag doll."

Samuel's eyes widened when he described the moment when his face was very close to the surface of the water. The way he spins a yarn is always both hilarious and amusing. You have the feeling with our gracious host that he has been on many adventures during his time, and we are all drawn into his stories with a smile on our faces.

"After that, I was hooked. I must have hurtled through the air thirteen or fourteen times in different places."

With a grin, Samuel puffed again on his soon-to-be extinguished cigarette.

After the lunch break, Samuel proposed an idea to the five of us horse riding students.

"Here's an option, if you want to go, we can take you on a horse tour through the forest. It's 500 pesos (3,000 yen) per person. What do you say?"

Of course, without hesitation, we were all up for it. From my viewpoint, I was the one who was looking forward to this tour the most. This is why I came here. To do things that are totally unobtainable in my everyday city-dwelling life. So, having become Samuel's disciples, Lavanya, David, myself, Axel, and

Anna started to head towards the striking mountain before us, with Samuel in the lead.

"The horses don't like to run on the ranch, as they can feel trapped there. The horses love to run free in the mountains."

Samuel had said this many times during his dressage lessons. He says that the horses are "doing their job" when they are walking within the confinements of the ranch. But going into the mountains is a reward for the horses, as opposed to a tedious service. For the horses, the grounds of the ranch are like a "workplace" or "office" for a businessman, and the forest is like a breathtaking haven, free from the confines of a cramped space. The six horses chosen for the ride, led by Samuel, walked slowly, without hesitation in a line towards the forest.

Ten minutes after we left the ranch, we entered the deep forest of Chiapas, where a throng of trees dominated the scene. Once in the mountains, however, I realized that this was very different from the horseback riding I had experienced in other tourist destinations, where the horses walked slowly along a predetermined track. There are naturally fabricated paths in the forest, but they are rather narrow, barely wide enough for a horse to pass through. In addition, the going is quite fast. Samuel was in the lead, followed by Lavanya and David from San Francisco, me from Japan, and the two Swedes bringing up the rear. The six horses move forward as if obsessed, weaving through the trees, stepping on grass and dead leaves as they advance. I found it very clear that my four-legged partner for the day was enjoying itself as I saw the joy in Neirida's eyes from where I was perched on her back.

As I clung fiercely onto the saddle with one hand and gently onto the reins with the other, I listened to the soothing sound of the wind and the dry crunch of hooves on dead leaves that had fallen from high above. We continued to follow the winding route accompanied by the consistent audibility of the trampled upon leaves. When I glanced up to check on our progress, Samuel was out of sight. I struggled to keep up with David and his partner, a black mare called Kimby, who was just ahead of me. I felt uneasy only being protected by my riding helmet, high up on a horse's back on a rugged mountain. There were many chilling moments when I almost lost my balance.

When the distance between Neirida and the horse in front opens up, she suddenly starts running to catch up. Neirida also speeds up suddenly when going down a hill. While we were descending a beastly path in the forest, there was a noticeable distance between the horse's back and the ground thanks to my sitting height and the slope of the mountain. It was easy to imagine that if I didn't desperately hold onto the saddle each time we went down the slope, I would fall and hurt myself. The path was narrow, with tree branches repeatedly heading towards my face. During our morning training, we had been taught a very practical method of how to duck our heads down to avoid the branches when they appeared in front of us. If I hadn't practiced this beforehand, I imagined my face would have been clean-shaven by a protruding branch with its sharp leaves, before eventually falling off my horse.

Another horse situation to be mindful of was when we were walking slowly along a flat road. If I wasn't alert to what Neirida was doing, she would suddenly stop and begin to pluck grass from the ground and eat it. Once this started she would continue to eat the grass until I pulled up on the reins and gave her a loud signal to "walk". With their flat teeth, they easily pluck the grass that is stuck to the ground, which would be difficult for a human to pull out with both hands. The clearly audible munching sound the horses made while they were enjoying their meal was quite eerie. This surprised me. The fine muscles of the horse's jaw and cheeks are designed to tear and chew any grass they find. And that they did.

Twice, while walking or cantering through the forest, I lost sight of the two Swedes who were supposed to be following behind me. There were so many trees in front of us and behind us, weaving our way through the forest, that it was easy to lose each other.

"David, our Swedish friends are having problems keeping up."

As I shouted out, David, who was trying his best to imitate Clint Eastwood in his prime, even though the going was tough, managed to inform Samuel of this. The first time he slowed down a bit, with Axel and his true love following behind me. But a short time after, it seemed that Samuel didn't want to wait for the two Swedish lovebirds who were trying to keep up with me. Later I found out why he hadn't stopped. This narrow path in the forest was actually a loop, which naturally led us back to where we started.

Samuel, Lavanya, David, and I met the two slowcoach Swedes, who by some forest miracle were waiting for us in a little open space with some tree stumps, where their horses stopped heading forward. Both horses were so busy eating grass that they totally ceased listening to the instructions of the not-so-superior humans above them.

Thrilling and exhilarating at the same time, this horse riding tour through the forest lasted about an hour and a half. The sun was beginning to set. On the gravel road from the mountain back to the ranch, Samuel, who had dismounted from his horse, said to us.

"You have to do a lot of riding before you can become a true master. Well, let's see, a hundred times. You'll probably fall off three or four times in that time. That's how you get better."

It would be fun to ride a horse a hundred times, but falling off multiple times doesn't appeal so much, I thought to myself remembering the thrilling, hair-raising time in the forest. If I really fell, I could injure my back and I would be unable to move, possibly even be trampled by a horse coming from behind. But despite these risks, the time I spent in the forest with my partner Neirida was a wonderful experience, regardless of what she thought of me. It's a once-in-a-lifetime opportunity to ride around on the back of a horse in the beautiful virgin forest of Chiapas.

After the day's session, the couple from Sweden headed back to San Cristobal, where they were staying. I was sure that the experience of this Evergreen Ranch would spread slowly but surely as they continued with their travels.

Lavanya and David went back to their room while I made my way to my lodgings to have a shower. This time Samuel chopped and burned the wood for me. The hot steam filled the compact shower room in the cool evening air. Of course, I was able to remove all the mud that had stuck to my feet in the swamp.

The shared kitchen of the hut.

-16-

French Mother

When I came back to the main house after changing, Stephanie asked me how my session had been and I told her it had been quite interesting, both in the mountains and in the mud.

"You went into the mud? That's crazy."

She sighed and shook her head, looking unimpressed. I thought I should defend Samuel.

"It was crazy, but it was fun."

Stephanie seems to be unaware of the details of how Samuel teaches.

For dinner that evening we were joined by Stephanie's mother, Christine, and her eldest daughter, Zoë, who had picked Christine up in San Cristobal. Zoë was a lovely girl with dark hair and big eyes. At sixteen she appears to have the strength of an independent adult but at the same time the expression of a young teen. Of course, she spoke English, French, and Spanish fluently, so I spoke to her in Spanish. The two girls, who have been brought up with people from all over the world from a young age, are not shy around visitors who come to stay with them, and they are friendly and polite when anyone talks to them. Thanks to the education they have received at home from their parents and the environment of the ranch, they do not have the typical teenage attitude of disliking the countryside. On the contrary, they have respect for nature.

Zoë's grandmother, Christine, had traveled from Lyon, France to see her daughter and grandchildren. She only speaks French, so Stephanie took over the translation for my conversation. Although she is already in her late sixties, she appears younger. She wears black-rimmed glasses that make her look stylish. Christine looks just like Stephanie when her smile reveals her white teeth. She is full of vitality.

Christine is trying to master Spanish because she comes to Mexico frequently these days. French and Spanish indeed have the same Latin roots, so they may be a little easier to learn if you are fluent in one of them, but I respect her unconditionally for trying to learn a new language at over 60 years old. We talked for a long time about our lives in France, Japan, and Mexico, so much so that Stephanie, our interpreter, had to interrupt us to say "I'm a bit tired, let me take a break". We got to know each other well and exchanged "Messenger" accounts so that we could keep in touch after the trip. She is very fond of hosting students from around the globe in her house in Lyon. It made me extremely proud when she informed me that her favorite visitors were from Japan, due to their respectful and polite manner. She showed me some photos of her trip to Japan when she was invited to my home country by one of them. She said if I came to France one day, I would be welcome in her home. Now I have a mother in France too.

"By the way, how did you find out about the ranch?"

Aunt Christine (I think of her as a family) asked me the same question I was asked by Lavanya the day before. It seemed unusual for a Japanese person to go through the difficulties in arriving at this particular ranch in Chiapas, where there are so many other famous and attractive places to visit.

"I saw it in a magazine and it was written about very favorably as a hidden gem."

While translating my words into French, Stephanie proudly showed her the magazine. It's the same one I've been carrying around with me.

"Woo la la! They are beautiful pictures. Oh, look, Zoë and Cheyenne are here too."

While Aunt Christine was looking through the magazine, I asked Stephanie to tell me how the magazine came to feature the ranch.

"When we first started taking guests to the ranch, we weren't booked up all the time like we are now. Three years ago I approached a publisher to see if there was any way we could appear in the magazine. They said yes, and within a short time a writer and a photographer were on their way."

I used to think that this kind of magazine had correspondents who traveled to different areas and introduced the hidden spots that they had discovered in their publication. But when it came to the Evergreen Ranch, it was the magazine that had been found by Stephanie.

A fun fact about Aunt Christine is that she also rides horses. She was trained in Lyon, France. She started learning to ride at the age of fourteen, which makes her a veteran of fifty years of experience. Thanks to her father, who took her to a riding club every weekend, she has a first-class riding license. Unfortunately, I wasn't able to see her skills during my stay, but Stephanie showed me a video she had taken of her mother a short time ago with her cell phone. It showed her maneuvering the horse in a relaxed manner, moving her upper body up and down in rhythm with the horse's gait. She was going around the track at a "trot," or a fast walk, one gear up from a slow walk. In one amusing part of the video, Christine was attempting to mount her horse. Aunt Christine's left foot was in the stirrup that she would use to help hoist herself up onto her majestic beast. She then grabbed the saddle for more leverage and tried to straddle the horse's back. But no matter how hard she tried, she couldn't lift herself, jumping, failing, pulling, failing, hoisting, failing, time after time. Stephanie sat next to me, watching her mother's ridiculous gestures over and over again, laughing for the longest time.

From left to right: Aunt Christine, Stephanie, Samuel, Cheyenne, and Zoë. Happily together for Christmas.

-17-

Mountains, Radio Waves and a Love Letter

There is no mobile phone signal around the Evergreen Ranch. However, there is a WiFi modem installed in the main house, so we can just about use the internet when we are inside, due to the connection being limited and unstable. So the family uses a messaging app called "WhatsApp" to communicate with friends through voice messages and texts. But as an office worker in a big bad city, I can't help checking my phone at least once a day, even on my days off, to make sure there are no important messages or missed calls. City dwellers, such as I, require the World Wide Web.

So the day I arrived, I was asking Stephanie where I could get a connection. It turned out that there was only one spot in the village where there was a good signal. This location was by a huge tree in the mountains. I imagined climbing up the tree with my mobile phone and witnessing a group of villagers sitting on the branches, talking to family and friends way up high. In my imagination, there were ladders at the foot of the tree to make it easier to climb, and parents and children were sitting side by side on the thicker branches, dangling their legs as they talked.

"All the people in this village go up the hill to that big tree and make a phone call."

After informing me of this, Stephanie handed me a map on a piece of straw paper that had the way from the ranch to the celebrity hill drawn on it. This is where I would find the all-powerful tree. It's a fifteen-minute walk from the Evergreen Ranch, she says, but the only landmarks seem to be a small stream and a church.

It was going to be hard to find, but that evening I set out to locate the magic tree that would permit me to connect with the outside world. As I left the ranch, I found myself on a gravel path lined with large cedar trees on either side, wide enough for two cars to pass each other. It's a chilly December evening in the highlands of Chiapas, and as I walk along the empty road, I feel more than a little lonely, I feel anxious. Of course, if you get lost, there is no mobile phone connection to call for help. The cold wind is rustling the grass and leaves, the sun is slowly setting and it is getting darker. Cars and motorbikes passed me three times on the way. All of them, going by their appearance, are driven by local men. They drove at a slow speed on the gravel road, and when their eyes met mine, they always greeted me with a gesture of palm up to their face.

"I'm looking for a big tree with a mobile phone signal. Do you know of any?"

I stopped one of the guys on a bike and asked him as I wanted to make sure I was going in the right direction.

"Hmm. Sorry, but I don't know about that."

He looked apologetic as he got back on his bike. He seemed to be from a neighboring village, unaware of this natural phenomenon.

Stephanie told me that there was a stream, so I looked for it, but all I could find was a trickle of water that was almost at an end. The map said there was a bridge over it, but there was no bridge in sight. All I could see was a puddle of water lying sadly at the side of the road. To reassure my mind, I told myself that this was the right direction, and I set off for the church. Stephanie's homemade map highlighted this area as a key point. It seemed that if I made the right turn, I would be able to reach the "magic tree" where I would receive the signal. After walking like those guys in the Olympics for a while, I finally found the church, a plain white building, hutesque in fact. At first glance, I could barely tell it was a church. The revealing factor was the discreetly displayed cross. I decided to go on believing that it must be so. By going right at the Y-junction, I should soon reach my destination.

Again I was moving fast when a group of about four local women, walking toward me in a line passed me. They all had their long hair tied up tightly and were wearing matching black skirts and blue blouses, so I guessed they were probably going to a Christmas mass. Just passing people made me feel a little less anxious. There was life in this wilderness. With each step, it was getting darker and darker. The cold wind that suddenly appears makes my shoulders tighten.

After a short walk, I came to a road lined with about five small houses. On the doorstep of one of the houses, a small pig with a black-and-white braid pattern was tied to a rope and was moving around energetically. Between two of the houses, there was a steep slope leading up to the mountain. I thought it must be this way and started to go up, relying on the map. But I couldn't find the right tree. In the rugged mountains of Chiapas, impressive trees are everywhere. Stephanie told me that I would find it very easily, but just before I turned off into a narrow mountain road, I felt uneasy and turned back towards the houses where I asked a woman who was drying clothes in her backyard, and also a girl in another yard, where I could find the tree with a telephone signal.

"Oh, a mobile phone signal right? Just go up here and you'll find it."

The directions were quite sketchy: just keep going up the road you're on. Everyone was looking at me suspiciously, wondering how on earth this Asian guy got here and what the hell did he want to talk about on the phone. Was he scouting for land to open up a chain of sushi restaurants? Maybe it was the look on my anxious face that puzzled them so much.

As I turned onto the mountain road, the houses disappeared and I kept walking along the side of a cornfield for about ten minutes. Just as I was about to give up on the idea, and go back to the ranch, a heavenly single bar appeared on my phone indicating mobile phone reception was at hand. Eventually, the otherworldly tree appeared safely in front of me. There were none of the lively social gatherings of villagers that I had expected. There was no one there but me. Only a black butterfly fluttered by a small pale yellow flower in the wild grass. But there was definitely a mobile phone signal, albeit a weak one. The tiered display of bars steadily rose from two to three. After my epic pilgrimage to the giving tree, I found that there were no messages or missed calls. C'est la vie. There was a funny feeling of unease when I wasn't within touching distance of radio waves or the all-important internet, even on holiday. As it turned out, I needn't have worried.

The sun was starting to set and the wind was getting colder, so I wanted to go back to the ranch. But I said why not take a look around at the view from the mountain seeing that I was here. From the mountainside, which overlooks a valley of cornfields, the awe-inspiring red sun is slowly setting. I crouched down at the foot of the magic tree admiring the contrast between the dark green of the trees and the red of the great ball of fire.

As the sun was setting, I hurried back to the ranch, eager to boil some water in the shared kitchen for a cup of tea. I didn't use water from the water server, but boiled water from the tap in a kettle. I had heard from Stephanie on my first day that the water from the tap was hard water but very tasty. I placed my novel along with my teacup on the wooden table and waited patiently for the water to reach boiling point. I took Stephanie's hand-written 'Radio wave searching map' out of my backpack and placed it on the table when I noticed a scrawl on the back. I had been focusing so hard on the front of the map, trying to decipher it, that I hadn't seen the back until now. There were three red biro hearts, drawn by an unknown local artist, and a man's name,

"José, Te amo (I love you)."

Maybe it was Zoë, maybe it was Cheyenne, or maybe it was a girl from the neighborhood who scribbled it down and left it behind. But even with such a romantic message, it was just a piece of notepaper to Stephanie, the quick-witted landlady. I looked at the back and the front and laughed out loud.

Hand-drawn map to the big magical tree.

-18-

At One with Horses

After enjoying a much-needed hearty meal in the main house with the family, I slept soundly in my glacial hut den, with the blankets pulled up to just below my eyes. My muscles were starting to ache in my back and thighs due to all the riding and walking. But, I have to say, it was pleasant exhaustion.

When the new day arrived, it was a crisp, cold Christmas Eve morning in the barn-like hut. By this time though, my sore throat had disappeared and I pushed open the door to the adjoining shared kitchen, feeling refreshed and a little peckish. However, after entering the kitchen I felt something was not quite right. The day before, I bought three small loaves of homemade brown sugar bread at a nearby shop to enjoy later. Also on offer in this fun-sized establishment were items, such as flavorsome chemically laced cup noodles and soap. During this particular visit, only the delicious-looking bread enticed me. On returning to the ranch, I tied the mouths of the bags together to prevent insects from getting in and put them on the highest wooden shelf. But at some point during the night they had been torn open with what appeared to be animal teeth, and the bread had been picked out and reduced by about half.

The first thing that came to my mind was the chickens that were always walking around the ranch on red alert for food. After all, the large window frame in this kitchen has no glass, and there is practically no barrier between them and the outside. It's high but tempting enough for a curious chicken with a bit of jumping ability to sneak in. They are also very active, screaming "Morning has come, get up!" even when it is still dark, and waking me up several times before my beauty sleep has been fulfilled. But if it had been the chickens, I would have noticed the rustling of wings and clucking in the kitchen next door even though I was in the land of nod.

My next thought was rats. The fact that I hadn't been awakened in the middle of the night by the noise in the kitchen next door, and the teeth marks on the bag, made me think that this was a strong possibility. There is an abundant amount of livestock on the ranch, but there is also a profusion of wildlife that are active at night. In the kitchen, where there was no fridge, I felt sorry for myself for being the victim of brown sugar bread theft. No doubt it was a feast for the crafty creatures guilty of the crime. I put the leftover bread in the food waste basket and closed the lid. Then, I put the torn plastic bags in a large jute bag specially used for plastic so that they can be recycled. Sadly, many humans believe that the world revolves around us, but we are kept alive by the relationships we have with other living beings, and the blue planet itself.

On Christmas Eve, my dressage master Samuel asked me what I wanted to do today, and I requested him to teach me how to "gallop". Galloping is the way a horse moves its legs when running at full speed, and in Japanese, it is called "Shu-ho". I had ridden horses and galloped at various tourist spots many times before, and I had never forgotten how exhilarating it was. What is more, I had ridden at a decent speed on the forest tour the day before, and I had a feeling that I would be able to gallop without too much trouble. As Lavanya and David had arrived before me and were more experienced with horses than I was, they agreed to my proposal.

On that day, Samuel responded to this request of mine with a special guest teacher. It was his second daughter, Cheyenne. The daughters of the ranch have been riding horses since childhood, and it is now a natural part of their lives. That's why everyone in the family is an expert. And Cheyenne, at fourteen years old, completely outclasses us on horseback.

With a sharp, high-pitched kissing noise from Cheyenne's pursed lips, Dutchess, the only white horse on the ranch, began to walk as she wished and then slowly ran in a perfect circle around the track. "Light and smooth" are the best words to describe her graceful movements. The way she stopped, the way she sped up, everything was just like a supermodel on a catwalk. As for the three of us, after more than an hour of walking and riding in the mountains yesterday, we had expected the horses to be at our mercy. But we soon realized that this was only possible with Samuel in front of us to guide the horses. Even when I signaled by making a noise with my mouth or tapped my ride on the belly with both heels to encourage my nag to walk, she refused to budge.

I was a little disappointed that I couldn't really do anything because I had the illusion that I could ride on my own. I repeatedly held her belly between my legs and commanded my horse to "walk." After stopping and then starting for a bit, Samuel's efforts in talking calmly to the horse began to bear fruit. She finally started to walk freely. Cheyenne went with us around the track and she had to correct my way of holding the reins several times. It seems that I was pulling too hard.

As I was going through all of this, the horse, on what appeared to be a whim, suddenly picked up speed and started to run at full pelt around the track. At first, it was just a bit of a run, but then it seemed to get into the swing of things and speeded up to maximum velocity. Despite the horse's euphoria, I was caught completely by surprise and almost lost my balance as my upper body fell backward. I held on for dear life and as I rounded the final corner, some 200 meters in, a branch appeared in front of my face. I ducked down and was able to narrowly avoid injury. That was all well and good, but shortly afterward I almost slipped off to the left and all but fell off my horse. But to preserve my life I grabbed the horn of the saddle and managed not to fall off.

"It went well this time. But your balance was a bit off."

While Samuel was smiling and praising me, my heart rate was still beating like a drum. I was not just a little off-balance, I was ready to fall. Being thrown from a height of nearly two meters at such a speed, no matter how soft the ground might be, is bound to hurt. I seemed to have lost my flexibility from when I was a university student. And just before that Lavanya had fallen off her horse. I didn't see it directly because I was too busy with myself, but for a while, I saw her supporting her back with her hands.

So, in short, that day's session was a disaster for all three of us. The only positive thing that happened was that David was a bit better with the horse and managed to go around the track a few times without breaking his neck. But I could see the look on David's and Lavanya's faces throughout the session: "it wasn't supposed to be like this".

"You have to make it clear to the horse that you are the one giving the orders. If you don't, the horse will start drinking water and eating grass on its own."

Samuel said over and over again. The horses eating grass or having a cool sip of water was the least of our problems. It seems that when left to our own devices, the hierarchy between the horses and us students was rubber-stamped that day. Or was the natural order of things just following its intrinsic course? I guess I need to have ridden many times to conquer one of these mighty beasts and be confident in my ability to let the horse know how I feel.

Finally, Master Samuel straddled a horse, grabbed its mane with his hand, and began to give commands to the majestic creature. A sharp signal was emitted from deep within his stuntman frame. The horse began to move wildly as if it was dancing. It was a demonstration of Samuel's ability to control the horse at will. The three of us, who had already dismounted and were listening to Samuel's explanation, were treated to a dizzying array of stops and turns. The horse raises its front legs and then kicks its hind legs in a bouncing motion, changing direction acrobatically over and over again. It reminded me of the wheelies and turns of motocross bikes I had seen on TV. The horse was completely at Samuel's mercy.

"You have to have a clear picture in your head of how you want to move, and you have to communicate that with cues, carefully chosen words, and by shifting your weight." We were overwhelmed by this spectacle as Samuel explained this to us.

This was the dramatic end of the three days of dressage lessons.

The young and beautiful master, Cheyenne.

Chapter five

Hallelujah

-19-

Siblings and Pine Cones

The main event of the day on Christmas Eve is dinner. I was invited to have dinner with fellow guests from different countries on this all-embracing scenic ranch. Before the festivities began, I had a couple of hours to kill, so I asked Stephanie if there were any other activities I could do, before the feast. She suggested going on a nature walk around the village and its surroundings, with a young boy from the village who acts as a guide. Guests from all over the world have been delighted to go up the mountain in the morning with the local boy and find rare mushrooms and learn about the plants. In a nutshell, it's an eco-tour. I only had an hour or so to walk around before dinner was served, so I knew I wouldn't have time to go into the forest and look for mushrooms. But it sounded more fun than just waiting around, so I decided to ask.

"There's a place on the top of a hill where you can get a nice view of the nearby town. It's only a twenty-minute walk from here."

Stephanie then began to give detailed instructions to the young guide, telling him to take this road and go up that hill.

My body still had some stamina left, so I was more than happy to stretch my legs to enjoy the great outdoors as well as get a feel for the village.

My chaperone was a well-tanned young chap called Chepe. Along with his younger brother Abel, he led me through the mountains outside the ranch, straddling and passing through fences along the way. I followed the two brothers, taking photos of the cornfields and the charming flowering plants with their attractive hues.

Chepe was thirteen years old and Abel was eight. Also in tow was Scooby, a small cream-colored dog who is the friendliest of the ranch's dogs.

As we paraded through the mountains on the unpaved earth, I found umpteen huge pine cones on the ground. On the highlands near San Cristobal, at an altitude of over 2,000 meters, there is a profusion of large pine trees due to its particular climate. I picked one up and put it in my backpack as a souvenir. After a while, Abel, who had been watching me, found an even bigger and prettier one and handed it to me.

"This is beautiful. Thank you." As we continued on our trek, Abel collected a few more pine cones that were about 20 centimeters long, so they filled up my backpack in a moment. Having so many of the cones, I thought that when I arrive back at the ranch, it would be a nice touch to put them in the main house as a natural Christmas decoration.

The walking tour turned out to be a pleasant stroll up and down the mountain paths, accompanied by Chepe and Abel who made sure I wouldn't get lost. As we walked along, I was chatting with them, asking them if they helped out in the fields or if they were tired of walking up and down hills with me. The boys seemed happy to show me around. They were great companions.

Whenever Chepe found a flower or a kind of nut, Chepe would tell me, "Look at that flower" or "You can eat that nut". Passing by a field of wax gourd or corn that suddenly appeared in the mountains, he would point them out to me. For the next hour we didn't come across another soul on the mountain road, nor did we see anyone working in the fields. It is a village with very few people, and it was Christmas Eve, so I imagined they were busy preparing dinner.

Chepe and Abel usually work with their family in the fields, so this landscape excursion is a part-time job for them when they have time.

"Puro trabajar (We work all the time)", Chepe told me as we walked, in his strong accented Spanish. His mother tongue is Tzotzil, the main language spoken in the nearby villages of San Cristobal. Luckily for me, he is bilingual and speaks Spanish fluently, the official language of Mexico. But he has a peculiar way of using words, always ending with the word "pues". For example, when he affirms "yes", he always says "sí, pues". It means "well, yes" or "well, that's the way it is". His brother, Abel, also adds "pues" to the end of his words, as to say "well" or "uh".

"Do you enjoy school?" "What's your favorite subject?" are questions that I'm sure I'd raise with children of these ages, and on several occasions, during our scenic trek, I was almost about to ask them, but swallowed the words, because maybe neither of them had even had a proper primary education. Many of the things that we Japanese take for granted might not be applied at all in Chiapas, especially in the villages outside the cities.

It was twenty-five years ago, so things may be different now, but I remember when I was a student I visited Amatenango village, known for its pottery about forty minutes away from Chichihuistan village. The children I met there, all-around ten years old, weren't on the hunt for candies or cola; the fact was they asked me for pencils. Unfortunately, I didn't have any pencils on hand, so I gave them a pen. I was more than a little surprised by their request, as I had never in my life had a lack of stationery. When I asked for a piece of paper to make some origami cranes to show the children, who had become my good friends, I was given a scrap of paper from a textbook, tattered and covered in pencil marks, which had been hunted down in the house somewhere after some discussion with their mother. The lives of the children in the villages scattered around this area are far from easy.

The three intrepid explorers, Chepe, Abel, and my good self walked around for an hour or so and before I knew it we were back at the Evergreen Ranch. During our walk, Chepe would say things to me like "look at that house". But in the end, I didn't see the beautiful view of the village up from the hill that Stephanie had told me about. Perhaps Chepe had taken me on a different route. I wasn't disappointed though, as I had thoroughly enjoyed my time with the brothers and what they had shown me along the way. I thanked them, gave them two hundred pesos, and bid them farewell. Stephanie doesn't charge a commission fee for this tour herself but had suggested to me before the three of us began our walk, that 200 pesos for their time would be fine. As a foreigner running a ranch, she may want to help contribute to the economy of the local villagers as much as she can.

Chepe and Abel posing in front of a cornfield.

-20-

How About a Sushi Roll?

When I returned to my secret hideaway, I found David and Lavanya's belongings strewn all over the place on the floor of the shared kitchen. Today was in fact, the day that Stephanie's best friend Matt, an Englishman, was coming to stay with them for Christmas. He would be staying at The Cottage, where David and Lavanya were residing. But David and Lavanya loved the ranch and wanted to stay longer than originally planned. Unfortunately for them, the rooms more desirable had already been claimed by myself and the new incoming guest, Matt. Therefore, the only option they had was to move into the barn-style hut. In this venue, I was on the right and David along with Lavanya were to slum it on the left. This space was not originally intended for paying guests, but for volunteer workers who now and then arrived to help out around the ranch. My room was more homely and comfortable, so the plan was that they would move in after I checked out the next day. I had shown the room to David and Lavanya the day before.

"This looks cool," they said, but not in their wildest dreams could these innocent friends have imagined how cold it would be at night after spending so much time by the warmth of the fireplace at their "Cottage".

Among David's luggage, there was a small guitar case. I recall seeing it when I first arrived and was curious about it. I love instruments and I play the guitar a little bit, so I couldn't resist asking David if I could twang the strings for a while. It was a small Californian gut guitar, just the right size for traveling. David and I talked about our guitar histories and showed off a little of our repertoire.

"I've only been learning to play the guitar for three years. I've never been very good at music, but I think it would be cool to be able to play some songs on the guitar once in a while."

David showed me a little arpeggio technique where he plucked the strings of his guitar with his fingers.

"It's called Hallelujah, you don't know this song?"

Honestly, I hadn't heard of it before. It was a slow-tempo song with a beautiful melody. As for me, I played a few blues and ragtime phrases that I had learned when I was a university student. Then I suggested it to David.

"Tonight at Christmas dinner, why don't we play some songs? You've got a nice guitar; it'll be fun for sure."

We all knew that Led Zeppelin wasn't getting back together any time soon, so why not?

"It sounds cool. Okay, let's do it."

David said he hadn't played in front of many people before, but he seemed to be game and agreed to take part. I've got a few songs in my repertoire that can enchant an audience, and knew I would regret not playing them. After this Christmas performance, the ranch would never be the same.

That evening, before dark, the main house was suddenly abuzz with activity in preparation for the party. In Stephanie's kitchen, the population density must have been the highest ever recorded in any kitchen within this village. Five members of the ranch family, including Aunt Christine, Matt, the English woodcarver, who had come to stay that day, and has known the family for 18 years, and Zoë and Cheyenne since they were small children. Joining in the fun were Sebastian, a German who runs a guest house nearby, his Mexican wife Julidia, and their three small children. Lavanya, David, and I were the other three guests. We took it in turns to use the kitchen, making salad and gracing the table with the food each one of us had prepared.

When Stephanie found out that I had returned from my walk with Chepe and Abel, she immediately asked me to help her. I hadn't heard anything about it until then, but she was going to make sushi rolls and I ended up as the new sushi MasterChef as I was the only Japanese representative of this international Christmas gathering. Even if I wasn't there, she had all the ingredients — seaweed, rice (Californian rice), sushi vinegar and the like — indicating that she wanted sushi on the menu.

"When I cook the rice, it ends up very dry," she said and asked me to tell her how to perfect her skills. Without a doubt, it helps to have some experience in this type of recipe preparation. I sometimes make sushi at home, but of course, they don't have a rice cooker at the Evergreen Ranch. However, when I was a university student, I sometimes cooked rice in a pot, and I also witnessed a friend make delicious rice in a kettle. The key is to add a lot of water and to keep the lid on from the beginning to the end.

"It's tempting to open the lid because you don't know what's happening inside, but never take it off. Be patient and don't let the steam escape."

Although I proudly announced this, convincing one and all that I knew what I was doing, the truth was that I was not confident at all because I had never tried to prepare this traditional Japanese dish before in another person's kitchen, with different pots and pans and stove burners. The heavy responsibility was beginning to weigh on my shoulders. Stephanie seemed intent on serving sushi rolls as one of the main dishes at their annual dinner for guests. Or perhaps she was planning this for weeks before since she knew that a Japanese guy was coming to stay with them and with no trouble at all to be able to help her.

I put the rice in an iron pot that had been washed in a colander along with some water and turned on the stove. Small beads of sweat began to appear on my forehead as I noticed there was a small gap between the pot and the lid, so it didn't fit snugly and the steam started to leak more than I expected. My heartbeat increased. Would I be asked to leave in shame before I could showcase my guitar shredding ability in the after-dinner show? Fear not, after some exchanges of opinions with Stephanie, we decided to put a wet cloth over the top to fill the gap. Fortunately, the lid was made of glass, so I could see what was going on inside. Once the water had evaporated and the steam had gradually died down, and I could no longer hear it simmering, I extinguished the flame. At that point, it was as good as done.

"Cover the rice with a lid and leave it for at least thirty minutes. That way the rice will steam naturally and become soft and fluffy."

This was my expert advice for Stephanie.

"That's the secret. Don't open the lid, use one and a half times as much water as the rice, and steam the rice at the end."

I was more than happy with my rice preparation explanation. Then I remembered that she was not only the co-owner but also the chef of the ranch. Stephanie was not someone who an amateur cook like me should be talking to about cooking.

I kept my fingers crossed that this pot of rice would turn out to be the greatest ever served in the Western Hemisphere. To my joyous relief, I managed to produce the rice to a level that would be acceptable to be served in Japan. Stephanie was well prepared with a bamboo mat for rolling the sushi rolls. I never found out where she got it. I filled a rectangular glass baking dish with a thin layer of steamed rice and sprinkled sushi vinegar evenly over the top. Stephanie and I took turns to fan the air with a white fan that she had in the house.

The non-traditional ingredients to roll were Philadelphia cheese, spinach, and canned tuna with mayonnaise. The rice was spread out on a bed of seaweed, with the ingredients evenly laid out on top of the rice. Then the rice was rolled in the bamboo mat. The problem was that I didn't have a sharp knife. The rusty petticoat knife provided was not sharp enough, and even when I dipped it in water, the seaweed and rice stuck to the blade, making it difficult to cut them into a round shape. But Matt, the Englishman who was observing the trouble I was having, found me a more appropriate blade to work with, and finally, I managed to make two dishes of sushi rolls. Lavanya, the Sri Lankan-American who was making a salad nearby, came up to me with a twinkle in her eye.

"It's been a long time since I've had sushi, so I'm excited."

She told me so, with her hair tied up in a red turban for the party that night. I imagined that she must have a much better palate than any of the poor Mexicans who suffer eating fake sushi in the chain restaurants in Mexico City, having eaten sushi in some of San Francisco's most fancy restaurants. However, I was almost done with my duties as a representative of fake Japanese chefs, so I didn't feel so much pressure from her words anymore. Rather, I was proud of the way I managed to prepare sushi rolls without the proper tools. The shape looked a bit squishy, but never judge a sushi roll by its configuration.

An impromptu sushi roll that I managed to make.

-21-

Christmas Tree

The kitchen and dining table in the main house were filled with friends who hadn't seen each other for a long time, eager to catch up with all the gossip they had missed. The newcomers like myself, David, and Lavanya were more than happy to mingle with them for the first time and listen to their stories. Zoë and Cheyenne had painted some pine cones and placed them around the fir tree that Samuel had cut from the forest to make a magnificent-looking Christmas monument. When the tree was placed on a wooden table it reached the ceiling. For my contribution at the base of the tree, I placed five large pine cones that I had picked up earlier, on my excursion with the boys.

Samuel placed blue illuminated lights around the tree to add to the ambiance. As we set up the tree, each of us magically produced a bottle of our favorite wine, chatting freely over a glass or two. I had asked Stephanie to ask her mom, who had been in San Cristobal the day before, to bring me back a Chilean Syrah on her return. After a while, it no longer mattered which wine anyone drank. The conversation was all over the place.

"When anyone asks them what their parents do, they say we are hippies."

Stephanie laughed out loud telling us so in front of Zoë and Cheyenne. I can understand this way of thinking. I can picture them as hippies at some stage in their lives. The children certainly have a funny way of describing their parents, but there is always a hint of respect behind it. Having a few more hippies in the world wouldn't be a bad thing if they turned out to be like this beautiful family.

Cheyenne, the second daughter, looks after Sebastian and his wife's children. As she has known them since they were babies, I can see that the children look up to her as if she were their big sister. It was then that I heard Cheyenne saying in Spanish to the three and five-year-olds: "Come on, we're going outside". For some reason, she was always speaking in English to me, so it was nice for me to hear her speak like a native Mexican. Then I saw her running around on the lawn outside the main house, laughing and joking with the young ones. For the first time during my visit, I saw that Cheyenne, who had always seemed so mature for her age, was in fact, still a young girl at heart.

By the way, Matt, the Englishman who had joined us at the lodge that day, is like a brother from another mother to Zoë and Cheyenne. The three of them interact so well together. Matt lives in Tulum, a small beach resort about an hour south of Cancun on the Yucatan Peninsula. For a living, he works with wood. One piece he created was a large, five-meter wooden sculpture for a trendy hotel there. Matt showed me on his mobile phone some of the motifs of the objects he has created, including a mermaid, a tropical bird, and a monkey.

"I'd like to live in Chiapas, but my work sells best in quaint resorts like Tulum. So I think I'll be working there for a while yet."

Previously, Matt lived with Stephanie and her family on another ranch in Chiapas for a year and is something of a relative now. At some point, he moved back to the UK for family reasons, but his passion for Mexico was so strong that he decided to make his home here again.

"I hope that one day I can come back to Chiapas and live near these guys."

It seems that the wild and warm charm that is not readily available in England inevitably attracts Matt.

Zoë, the eldest daughter at sixteen, joins me and Matt. While chatting with Zoë and Matt, the topic of Japanese animation soon pops up. They started talking about their favorite Hayao Miyazaki films, telling how much they liked "Spirited Away", or how cute "Totoro" was. I could only recommend the earlier film by Miyazaki "Nausicaä of the Valley of the Wind" as they knew more about it than I did. In the last decade or so, it seems that the way people around the world view the Japanese and our culture has changed. It's not only Kawasaki motorcycles or whatever happened to JVC that people are interested in these days. What is more, even though we are in the heart of the Mexican countryside, one of the main dishes for dinner is my world-famous sushi roll.

When I first arrived in Mexico 25 years ago, there was no internet and the only Japanese words Mexicans knew were "Geisha", "Samurai", "Hara-kiri" and "karate". The average Mexican barely knew the word "Ninja". When the kids in my neighborhood saw me, they ran away in fear that I would karate chop them. The only choice of anime that was available at that time was the classic Japanese anime, "Heidi of the Alps" which was first released in Japan in 1974. It turned out to be quite popular here.

Nowadays, most people are familiar with classic anime such as "Dragon Ball " and "Captain Tsubasa". Even if they are not shown on TV in Mexico, thanks to the internet, it is possible to watch anime that is shown in real-time in Japan, with Spanish subtitles. J-pop is also popular. Once I met a teenage boy who happened to be a fan of Ikimono Gakari. And even those who are not particularly interested in Japan are beginning to realize that there is more to Japanese cuisine than just sushi and tempura. These things not only make me feel much more at home but fills me with pride as well.

The preparations for the bring-your-own party are almost complete.

-22-

Hallelujah

As nightfall was upon us, the dinner kicked off with Samuel's toast of "Merry Christmas". We had already been drinking wine while preparing the meal, so it was a lively affair. Aunt Christine doesn't speak English and Samuel's Spanish is quite broken. So Stephanie and her daughters stepped up with their superior language skills, and we entered a borderless situation where three languages, including French, were intertwined.

The youngsters start fighting over the sushi rolls I've made with all the energy of an athletic meet when the gun goes off. It was an honor and a privilege to see the slightly misshapen sushi rolls disappear from the two plates so quickly. Not only the sushi but Laverna's salad was also eaten with chopsticks.

One of the guests on the day, Sebastian, a German who came from Europe and fell in love with the area, now runs a guest house with his Mexican wife, Julidia. They have a son and daughter in kindergarten as well as a baby boy. Sebastian, who sported a hunting cap, took pictures of the party with a very robust SLR camera. His wife was wearing a traditional hand-woven Mexican dress. The fried tacos she brought were authentic as can be. For a bonus, Julidia spoke French. The music played was a random selection of Western music from the seventies, with a focus on lively songs such as Queen's Bohemian Rhapsody. The DJ in resistance was Samuel, who, at fifty-eight years old, was just ten years older than me, but his taste in music made it even easier to identify his generation.

As the meal was winding down, Samuel suddenly called out to everyone.

"I heard that Shiniji plays the guitar. Let's have him play for us."

David had told Samuel that we were each going to perform a song. I, who Samuel still calls "Shiniji" with an additional "i" added to my real name, only had two self-made lyric cards with chord progressions. David was on standby with his trusty guitar. In the afternoon we turned the shared kitchen into a hastily built studio for a quick rehearsal for the night's extravaganza. I played a few chords and found the guitar to be in perfect tune.

The silence was blinding, with everyone's attention focused on me. Taking the situation by the horns, my first song was, "Miagete Goran Yoru no Hoshi wo" by Kyu Sakamoto. I was not familiar with the original version, but after hearing Ken Hirai, a present-day pop singer cover it in 2003, I added the song to my hit list.

"This song was a hit in Japan in the 1960s and it's about the stars in the night sky that light up the happiness we have. It reminded me of the stars on view here, and I thought it was perfect for today."

I was the only one here who understood Japanese, so I explained a bit in English and then started to play the guitar. The lyrics go something like this in English.

見上げてごらん夜の星を

(Look up at the stars at night)

小さな星の小さ光が

(Small lights of little stars)

ささやかな幸せを歌ってる

(Are singing us a little happiness)

見上げてごらん夜の星を

(Look up at the stars at night)

僕らのように名もない光が

(The nameless stars like us)

ささやかな幸せを 祈ってる

(Are wishing us a little happiness)

I'm not a professional singer at all, but if the opportunity arises to open my vocal cords then there's no holding me back. One thing is for certain, even if I'm not very good, my audience will never forget it. That night, already drunk on wine, I was able to sing quite comfortably and without making any mistakes. My captive viewers refrained from singing along with me, due to the fact it was in Japanese. However, when I finished the song they banged on the tables and cheered wildly. I was worried that they wouldn't like it and was relieved by their energetic reaction.

With the concertgoers in my back pocket, I was full of confidence. The second song I chose was "Tu Carcel (Your Prison)" by a Mexican singer, Marco Antonio Solis. This tune was a big hit in Mexico and is loved by all generations; it has been played on the radio for a number of years. Even though this song is more than twenty years old, I still hear it played from time to time.

It's a classic Mexican love song about an ex-girlfriend who gives up on the poor protagonist and moves on to be with a richer man. I choose this song not because of pure reasons such as the lyrics, but for technical reasons: its narrow vocal range used for singing makes it easy for me as an amateur to sing. Anyway, there are so many songs in Mexico about breaking up and not breaking up.

While I was singing, those in the drunken crowd who knew it sang along. The first song was in Japanese, so it was quiet, which made this time even more lively. Even David, an American who I would have thought unlikely to know it, after glancing at my lyric card sang along happily. I felt a bit sorry that I hadn't prepared more songs for them to enjoy. I'm sure they felt the same. My biggest weakness is that I have trouble memorizing the lyrics of any song, so I can't sing a song without looking at the lyric card with the chord progression. Now, with my momentum in full flow, and the spectators behind me, I launched into another track, "You're My Sunshine" with some random accompaniment. It is really a very simple short tune, but I couldn't get the words out before the second verse, so I just hummed along and everyone sang out loud. Freddie Mercury would have been proud.

After my incredible performance, I passed the guitar to David, expecting him to follow me, but he just put it up against the wall. He whispered to me, "I'll take my turn in a moment", and took a few sips of wine. I couldn't blame him really. I'm sure even the best of them, Bruce Springsteen, Mick Jagger, and Elton John, to name but a few would be hesitant to follow my electrifying act. Maybe he needed time to prepare in his own way. We chatted for a while, nibbling on side dishes, and then David started to play his song "Hallelujah" on his guitar. The whole house went quiet. The chords spread slowly and steadily in the dry air of the room,

That night, the table in the main house was full.

and I was instantly reminded that this was a holy night. David and I had shown each other what pieces we were going to play in the afternoon. At that time I had only heard the first part of the song, so it was the first time I had heard the full chorus.

It begins with the words "David played a secret chord to please the lord", a mysterious lyric of some significance, with a quietly soothing arpeggio that fits perfectly.

I later found out that "Hallelujah" was written by Leonard Cohen and was released in the 80s. Many artists have covered it since then, becoming a hit each time. Due to this, it is loved by all generations. The catchy phrase "Hallelujah" is repeated four times at the end of the song, so there is always a big chorus. Even non-English-speaking Aunt Christine and I, who were unaware of this song, can sing along with the chorus. The song contains four verses. The second and third verses are sung solo by Zoë, the eldest daughter, using the spoon I gave her as a microphone. She sang it beautifully with so much confidence. The fourth and final verse was sung by David, the real star of the show. When David finished playing the last chord, there was a moment of silence. Then came the huge cheers of appreciation. David had given us a grand finale. After the show, lively conversation resumed, and everyone was enjoying the afterglow of the musical performance.

David and I, feeling relieved, drank a lot of wine. Latin dance music was being played and the dancing began. Stephanie and Samuel's daughters, Zoë and Chayanne, are half American and half French, but they grew up in Mexico, so the Latin influence in their lives made them quite flexible and rhythmical in their steps. I accompanied Samuel onto the dance floor next to the dining table, where he danced with his eldest daughter, Zoë, and I cut the rug with Cheyenne.

It was my first visit to the Evergreen Ranch and I was so happy to get to know and be welcomed by everyone. Later that night, as I danced with Samuel and Lavanya, I began tapping on the Christmas feast table, getting into the rhythm of the music. Due to the wine kicking in, some parts of the night were hazy. Later, I found out that my John Travolta moves had been recorded by Aunt Christine who was filming me. This is how my Christmas Eve at the Evergreen Ranch went by, with a global combination of people, international food, and music.

As the esteemed guests slowly left the party, I decided to leave the main house to go back to my cabin. While crossing the wide grassy meadow, I saw Samuel and David talking quietly around an inviting fire. There were no street lights visible. Only a soft yellow glow leaking from the main house was detectable. Thanks to the natural light emitted from the stars and the moon, darkness was kept at bay. In the silence the flames crackled, danced, and burned, casting black shadows across their deep-set faces. We said goodnight and I continued my walk across the grass, hearing nothing but my own footsteps.

Zoë sings Hallelujah.

-23-

The Morning the Journey Ends

It's a little after eight o'clock on Christmas Day morning and I'm all packed up and ready to go back to Mexico City. As usual, there are cats waiting for me in front of the main house, looking for the chance to infiltrate the house. I managed to block them with my foot and slip through the door, entering alone into the main house. Stephanie, who had looked after me for three days, made me my last breakfast. I also said "Good morning" to Samuel, who had just woken up and was even more shaggy-haired than usual.

I asked for some fruit, yogurt, crepes, and coffee for breakfast. In the chilly morning air of the highlands, the steam from the Chiapas coffee puffed up against my nose.

Before departing, I paid for the wine I had ordered during my stay and for the horse-riding tour to the mountains. I had brought some extra cash as I had been told in advance that I could not pay by credit card. Stephanie checked with Samuel how much I had to pay for the dressage session to add to my bill. After paying her in cash, I was debt-free. I have a habit of asking for receipts on every trip, just in case. But the Evergreen Ranch doesn't have a standardized receipt issued by their accounting system. So Stephanie wrote down the cost of my stay on a plain piece of white copy paper and signed it at the bottom.

> San Cristobal de las Casas
> Evergreen Ranch
> 25 December 2018
>
> 3780 pesos for accommodation,
> meals, and equestrian activities
>
> Manager
> Stephanie d'Arregon

"I hope this will do. I put Stephanie, the manager, even though I don't have a job title or anything of the kind" she said, laughing cheekily. I laughed too.

"I just like the word 'manager' so when I get the chance to use it I take it."

It seems that a traveler like me, who asks for a receipt, is few and far between on the Evergreen Ranch. The total cost of my four-day, three-night stay was about 22,000 Japanese yen. Whether this was cheap or expensive was no longer important to me, as I had experienced so many new things during my time here. The memories will stay with me always.

After breakfast, I asked Stephanie to call a taxi for me. But the driver from the next village, whom she always calls up, didn't reply to her voice message. I had heard that he was a very responsible driver, but it was Christmas Day after all and I imagine that the majority of locals would have attended a party the night before. As Stephanie says, most of the villagers were still not awake. One option we had though was to ask Sebastian, a German who had come for Christmas dinner the day before, to help me out. He was going to San Cristobal that day on an errand and Stephanie asked if I could join him. Sebastian said he was taking three German guests who had been staying at his house to San Cristobal that morning.

Stephanie sent a voice message from her mobile phone and waited for a reply, which came shortly afterward from Sebastien.

"Of course, I'll be happy to give him a ride. I'll be setting off at 10:30."

But I had already prepared myself to leave earlier, so I didn't want to wait for another hour. Besides, it would be risky to arrive at the airport without no extra margin of time, as it was the last day of a four-day long weekend. We were both thinking about it when Stephanie, on the spur of the moment, went outside and soon returned with a taxi behind the main house. She had managed to stop the taxi on the road by the ranch. It just so happened that the driver had just come from San Cristobal with passengers to a village just beyond San Isidro Chichihuistan, and was about to make the return journey alone. So, for 200 pesos, he would take me directly to San Cristobal. It was a bit more expensive than the taxi I had taken on the way to get to the ranch. But it was going to be much cheaper than the price of a taxi if I went to the nearest village, Betania, which costs 150 pesos, and then took another connection to San Cristobal. I decided immediately to take the ride on offer to San Cristobal. If I declined, the chances of catching another one soon were slim. After all, today is Christmas Day.

I didn't get the chance to say goodbye to Cheyenne, Zoë, and Aunt Christine who were still sleeping, as were Lavanya and David who had practiced riding with me for three days, or to our special guest Matt from England. But I'm sure we'll meet again one day.

I walked alongside Samuel and Stephanie from the main house while the driver brought the car around to the back of the hut where I had stayed for three days. Before leaving, Samuel told me to get on his green tractor. Then he took my camera in his hand.

"I will take a photo of you on the tractor of the ranch."

He pressed the shutter again and again, showing me the pictures he had taken. My feeling was that I looked shy and uncomfortable rather than happy on the tractor. After dismounting it, we hugged and said goodbye.

He said, "That was a great performance last night. I'll have a quality guitar waiting for you when you return for your next concert here. Before then, please practice some other songs."

I was flattered, but I just said, "Okay, I'll do it." Stephanie, who was talking to the taxi driver near the fence of the ranch by the road, smiled at me when she saw that I had said goodbye to Samuel.

"Did we pass the test? You'll bring your family next time, won't you?"

I laughed and said,

"Of course, I will. The next time you see me, I'll be with my family."

Then we said goodbye to each other and I got into the taxi. It felt like such a long time since I had been in a car and not on the back of a horse.

As I left the Evergreen Ranch and headed for San Cristobal, we drove slowly along the dirt road with sharp bends. Glancing out of the window I noticed the same wooden signs when I first arrived: "Speed limit 20 km /h. Over speeding is a fine of 1,000 pesos." The taxi turned into a boneshaker as it rattled across the countless tiny jagged stones strewn from here to there on the gravel road, just as it had done on the way there. I decided to sit in the back seat instead of my usual favorite passenger seat and watched in silence the scenery of the village where I had come to be familiar with and loved its people.

The car was already at the exit of the village of San Isidro Chichihuistan, and the houses were sparse when I saw an old man in very dirty clothes lying in the street, surrounded by four men.

"What's going on?" I asked the driver.

"Oh, he is just drunk. It was Christmas Eve yesterday, you know?"

The young taxi driver who came from two villages away from San Isidro Chichihuistan seemed to be wondering why I was interested in the incident.

"By the way, I heard that one of the men from this village was thrown in a local jail yesterday. He tried to touch a girl, but they stopped him."

It reminded me of the loud sermon from the church I had heard the night I arrived at the Evergreen Ranch.

"Don't drink too much. When you get married, you mustn't touch other women."

The pastor's gruff voice sounded like a gun in the unobstructed sky. If even in this particular village, a man can be caught drunk and messing around with a woman in a drunken stupor, then perhaps the pastor's sermon is sometimes necessary.

This is the whole story of the four days I spent at a ranch in the village called "San Isidro Chichihuistan". At first, I wondered why people from all over the world would come to this forest in the interior of Chiapas, but now I understand it.

"I got an email from Italy saying an Italian couple wanted to spend the New Year here."

On the last morning of my return to Mexico City, Stephanie was still rushing to respond to the requests for accommodation from repeat visitors to the ranch. For those who have been here before, the ranch is like a family home from home, one to which you can always return and be welcomed with open arms. Like the Italian couple, I started to think of a meticulous concrete plan in my head: "When can I come back again?"

After arriving in San Cristobal by taxi, I boarded a large coach for Tuxtla Gutierrez, where the airport was. I'd spent a little extra money than I had on the way there, but I'd managed to use reasonably priced transport. Additionally, I'd taken the liberty of declaring victory against the "challenge" from the ranch that had arrived before my trip. Back at home in Mexico City, at the tail end of the year, I was reminiscing about my time at the Evergreen Ranch with the melody of "Hallelujah" in my head.

Afterword

Over the years, I have visited many places for a vacation or on a business trip where I have encountered strange foods, cheerful and gloomy people, unusual landscapes that make me wonder how they came to be, and rhythmic and stirring music. I've been to seventeen countries in my lifetime. But it's not often that I get to travel beyond the level of personal memories, to the point where I want to share them with others.

"Mountains, Radio Waves and a Love Letter", is the story of my entire trip during the Christmas holidays of 2018, when I went to stay in a small village called San Isidro Chichihuistan in Chiapas. I didn't originally set out to write a book about it. It was just an experience so different from the rest of my travels that I started to write it down before I forgot about it. Once I started, I couldn't stop, and now it's been published as a book.

By the way, I am still in touch with Matt, the English woodcarver mentioned in the text. We once had a chat about why people from all over the world come to the Evergreen Ranch. Matt said it was "Quiet, wild, off the beaten track, semi-adventurous, fun, with a wholesome family. I think people come here for any of these reasons," he said. He is so good at describing things and gets straight to the point in a few words. As for me, I can't summarize like this, so I ended up writing an exceedingly long travelogue.

Most of the travel books I know are by young people traveling alone or are written by writers or celebrities. For a working person like me, travel is not an easy thing to do because of time constraints. But travel is still fun. Everywhere I go, I try to find out what the locals are eating off the menu, or discover hidden restaurants or places with great views. If you never give up and keep poking your head around, you'll occasionally come across a story like this one. Incidentally, this is the first time on our blue planet that a story set on the Evergreen Ranch has been published as a book. For sure, I wasn't the first person to visit this awe-inspiring destination, and I won't be the last. Nevertheless, it is a glorious feeling to be the world's first visitor to have this experience published in book form.

Before I finish, I would like to express my vast appreciation to the family of the ranch, Stephanie, Samuel, Zoë, Cheyenne & Aunt Christine, who took care of me from day one. Not forgetting the horses, sheep, dogs, cats, chickens, and the cowardly-looking turkey. Thanks also to Lavanya and David who I spent most of my time with, and everyone who was with me on Christmas Eve including Chepe and Abel who helped make the trip so unique. Finally, I would like to thank Paul for being my co-pilot on this literary adventure and adding a little salt to my English version of the book. I would like to take this opportunity to thank them all.

Shinji Yoshikawa

About the Author

Shinji Yoshikawa, born in Osaka in 1971, studied Spanish in Oaxaca, Mexico during a two-year break as a student at Tsukuba University, Japan. He experienced a "forced Latinization" of personality during the two years before returning to Japan. On his return, he completed his final year in Sociology gaining a bachelor's degree.

After graduating from university, he worked as a gem buyer, purchasing diamonds, pearls, opals, and other precious stones in India, Hong Kong, and other countries around the world. Subsequently, he moved back to Japan, where he worked as a sales representative for a Japanese magazine publisher selling advertising space and was a starting member of a new web marketing business. He is currently working for a Japanese food company in Mexico, where he is in charge of PR and advertising.

As a husband and father of two daughters, he is also responsible for preparing meals and cleaning up afterward on weekends. His specialty in cooking is oven-baked pork belly with tomatoes. Fascinated by travels and creative writing, he is always on the lookout for new destinations to explore between busy office working days.

He can be reached at shinjiyoshikawa1110@gmail.com.

Printed by Amazon Italia Logistica S.r.l.
Torrazza Piemonte (TO), Italy

61595198R00097